...and gorska made the pictures

The Internet for Your Kids

Deneen Frazier
Dr. Barbara Kurshan
Dr. Sara Armstrong

with contributions from
John Blackburn

SYBEX®

San Francisco • Paris • Düsseldorf • Soest

Associate Publisher: Roger Stewart
Acquisitions Manager: Kristine Plachy
Acquisitions & Developmental Editor: Sherry Bonelli
Editor: Kim Wimpsett
Technical Editors: Jeanie Graser and Dave Graser
Book Designers: Kate Kaminski and Caryl Gorska
Graphic Illustrator: Caryl Gorska
Electronic Publishing Specialists: Cyndy Johnsen, Kate Kaminski, Robin Kibby
Production Coordinator: Amy Eoff
Indexer: Nancy Guenther
Cover Designer and Illustrator: Caryl Gorska

This book is dedicated to the children who will discover how to grow, explore, and help others in the world. They are our teachers.

Acknowledgments

The authors would like to thank the following people:

Dr. Thomas Sherman at Virginia Polytechnic University for providing us with insight into what we know about how kids learn and how to use online services to support this learning.

Sherry Bonelli and Kim Wimpsett for working tirelessly at Sybex to develop a high quality guide for kids as drivers on the Information Superhighway. Technical editors Jeanie Graser and Dave Graser for reviewing the chapters and providing keen insight. The editorial and production team—Caryl Gorska, book designer and illustrator; Cyndy Johnsen, Kate Kaminski, Robin Kibby, electronic publishing specialists; Amy Eoff, production coordinator; Laura Arendal, revisor and editor of the previous edition; and Christian Crumlish, who wrote the glossary—for contributing their ideas and expertise toward creating the attractive book you hold in your hands.

Dr. Judi Harris, professor at the University of Texas at Austin, for her significant contribution to understanding, developing, and archiving educational networking projects. Her research has helped us shape the framework of this book.

John Blackburn for his contribution of creative ideas, quality writing, and enthusiastic support in making this book come together.

Barbara Martin for contributing her time and talent to help organize many of the details for book.

Also thanks to the creators of all of the Internet sites included in this book. All of you are truly expanding the ability of all kids to learn.

We are especially grateful to all of the kids who reviewed and tested the projects in this book. Their wide eyes and big smiles convinced us that this book would be a valuable tool for kids.

Contents at a Glance

Table of Contents

Table of Contents

Table of Contents

Foreword

Whether you are 10 years old or 75, a student or teacher, a youngster or parent, the Internet and World Wide Web provide you with extraordinarily rich opportunities for learning and growth. These dynamic mediums help you communicate, create, experiment, and explore on a scale so broad that you can travel electronically across the world and back again within minutes. Whether your passion is astronomy or zoology, you can use the Internet and the Web to access rich and relevant information; connect with resources located in Walla Walla, Washington, or Wanaka, New Zealand; and conduct conversations, ask questions, share stories, or collaborate on projects with peers, mentors, and experts from all over the world.

This awesome global reach is powerful in itself but is made more so by what it allows you to do locally: become a more engaged student, a more active and informed citizen, a more effective teacher, a more involved parent. Harnessing the potential of these global resources is what this book is all about. *The Internet for Your Kids* is a carefully selected collection of projects, games, and activities designed for learners of all ages. With the authors' careful guidance, you will learn how to use the Internet and World Wide Web to make global connections, express your opinions and ideas to people in leadership positions, challenge yourself intellectually, research information, and even create your own World Wide Web pages. In addition, you'll find practical information about how to get started on the Internet and the Web and how to separate the Web tricks from the Web treats. *The Internet for Your Kids* is a valuable jumping-off point for those new to the Web and the Internet, and it is a useful catalyst for further exploration for those more comfortable with these mediums.

What specifically makes the Internet and Web so powerful and exciting? Three attributes, it seems to us, underscore their potential value for all learners. First among these is the near immediate access to a world of information and to peers, experts, and mentors. Imagine a high-school student who is working on a school project about World War II. A few years ago, her research efforts would likely have centered around books and articles—valuable resources in themselves. Today, the Internet and Web can help enhance the depth and sophistication of her work: She can see documentary footage from the war, listen to speeches by leaders of both sides, and read full texts of the terms of surrender. If she becomes curious about a particular aspect of the War—say the first black fighter squadron—she can search out experts and even communicate with actual pilots through e-mail. In this process of accessing, analyzing, and synthesizing this rich information, she becomes an interactive learner. This, many education experts suggest, increases the likelihood that she will retain what she is learning well into the future.

A second powerful attribute of the Web in particular is its accommodation of a wide variety of learning styles. In contrast to a book, which presents information in text form, the Web is a multimedia environment—allowing for graphics, audio, and video in addition to text; as a result, each learner has multiple ways of accessing the information presented. This multimedia aspect of the Web also means that information presented is often more engaging—it literally leaps off the page—for all learners.

A third powerful attribute of the Internet and World Wide Web is the potential to break down many forms of isolation: Imagine a child who is alone in his class or family in being curious about dinosaurs, and he has already exhausted the school library's resources in this area. Internet and Web access offers him the possibility of connecting with peers who share his interest, as well as with paleontologists. Not only can he find company through these mediums, but, as his interest in dinosaurs finds an outlet, his curiosity may soar and encompass more information and connections. One day, because of these experiences, he may even become a paleontologist. Now, imagine a high-school science teacher whose passion for teaching and biology are limited only by her inability to find local colleagues with whom to share ideas that might improve her teaching. She can use the Internet and the Web to connect with science teachers from around the country and share ideas and strategies with her distant colleagues. Such communication can lead to collaboration between several science classes in different parts of the country in online science projects. Most of us, in fact, can likely benefit by connecting with others who share our interests, whether we are students, teachers, kids, or parents. By breaking down barriers erected by time and distance, the Web and Internet can help us make those connections.

Using the Internet and the Web to maximize our own potential as learners and as people is not always easy. The sheer volume of information available to us can be overwhelming. Thankfully, The *Internet for Your Kids* has done much of the sorting work and has produced this valuable collection of projects and activities. Resources like *The Internet for Your Kids* can help learners of all ages use the Internet and the Web to realize their own hopes and dreams, goals, and aspirations. That makes them powerful tools in education, at every level. As filmmaker George Lucas, the founder of The George Lucas Educational Foundation, has said, "There is a natural level of curiosity and motivation in every individual, and it is incumbent upon us to devise ways to tap into that creative energy to help students channel their excitement and ideas into productive educational experiences." Such is the benefit of *The Internet for Your Kids*.

THE GEORGE LUCAS EDUCATIONAL FOUNDATION

Located in Nicasio, California, The George Lucas Educational Foundation was founded in 1991 to explore the potential for technology and other innovations to revitalize public education. GLEF is sharing the results of its research with the recent release of Learn & Live™, a documentary film hosted by Robin Williams and a companion resource book. These materials address a broad range of issues affecting today's students and profile schools where innovative teaching, combined with effective uses of technology, makes learning meaningful and fun. An electronic version of the Learn & Live resource book can be found on the Foundation's Web site (`http://glef.org`), which also features audio and video clips from George Lucas and from experts in education; past issues of the Edutopia®, the Foundation's newsletter; and information about Foundation activities.

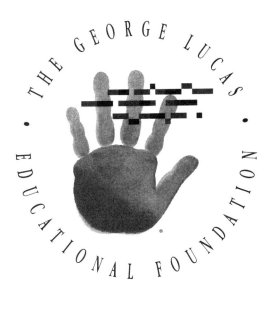

Introduction for Parents

You've listened to your kids' advice and purchased a connection to the Internet for the family...now what? It is like you've just turned on a fire hydrant and you are trying to fill a glass of water. Do you feel like your kid knows more than you? Do you feel that they are the "computer whiz" in the family?

Most parents do. And the answer is not for you to learn everything your kid knows, but rather to gather a few tools that give you and your child ideas for how to harness the power of this global technology so that you can enhance your own lives.

The Internet is ever-evolving, but one thing won't change—it's here to stay. Soon, your child will need to become familiar with the Internet to become successful in school and, eventually, in the workplace. This book is to give you and your kids some ideas for exploring the vastness of the Internet and discovering meaningful information, resources, and people.

Special Features of This Book

In Chapters 2–9, you will find projects that cover many different subject areas such as math, science, social studies, language arts, fine arts, and foreign languages. The projects will engage your child's imagination, personal interests, and questions about the world. The projects cut across subject areas so that your child can practice math skills without thinking of it as a math assignment.

Here are the special features of each project:

 Every project contains step-by-step instructions written directly to your child.

★ Every project culminates in a concrete and tangible product that your child creates themselves.

★ Every project has been tested by kids and revised according to their comments.

★ Every project directs kids to safe and appropriate sites that have been reviewed by teachers for kids to explore on their own.

★ Every project can be worked on by one child, several children, or children and parents together.

★ Every project introduces a handful of Web sites that are indexed in a summary list found in Appendix A.

This book also uses a few typographical conventions to make it as easy as possible to be online:

★ Words that your child should type in are in **bold**.

★ E-mail addresses and Web addresses are in a `monospaced font`.

★ New terms are displayed in *italics* (see the glossary in Appendix B for definitions of Internet terms).

What Is the Internet?

If you could take a picture of the Internet, you would see a spider web of connections between computers all around the world. With these connections, someone using a computer in Copenhagen, Denmark, can retrieve information from a computer in Chicago, Illinois, send information to a computer in Caracas, Venezuela, and validate information with a computer in Tokyo, Japan...all in about 10 minutes. It's faster than flying, and you do it from the comfort of your own home.

NOTE The Internet is also commonly referred to as the "Net." The "World Wide Web" or "Web" is actually a subgroup within the Internet.

You will learn about several different Internet tools in Chapter 1, *The World of the Internet*. These tools let you travel across the Web connections to find the computers that hold information about an area of interest.

NOTE Whether you're using a Macintosh or a PC with Windows, you'll be able to find software to connect to the Internet without a problem. In almost every town there is a local Internet service provider (ISP) that provides individual and family Internet accounts.

Why Write a Book for Kids about the Internet?

Before answering this question, ask yourself:

- ⭐ Who likes using computers?

- ⭐ Who is adventurous and curious?

- ⭐ Who has the time and the energy to explore the vastness of the Internet?

- ⭐ Who is the best teacher of technology?

The answer to all of these questions is *kids*! Kids of all ages are familiar with computers and are not afraid to push buttons and try new things.

This book will give you some ideas about where to direct your kids' curiosities and energy to learn new things, make new friends around the world, and contribute ideas toward making the world a better place. In addition, the book provides a hands-on approach to learning. This pedagogy will provide an exciting way to teach the applications and tools for the Internet.

Many books about how to use the Internet for personal and professional reasons are written for adults, but few with ideas about how to use and create on the Internet for learning and fun are written for kids.

Using This Book as a Guide

The Internet is far-reaching, and it changes too quickly to draw a map of it. This is a guide to a variety of resources and projects that are interesting and fun. Once you are familiar with the territory, you may not need a detailed guide but only specific addresses, which you can find in Appendix A.

This book is separated into nine chapters with each describing different sites and features of the Internet. Chapter 1 is about the Internet in general and will be helpful if you are new to the Internet.

Chapters 2–9 include projects that help you approach the Internet with a particular goal in mind. For instance, Chapter 2, *Making Global Connections*, includes projects to connect you in different ways with people around the world and help you communicate with them. Chapter 9, *Building Cool Sites on the Web*, includes projects that will help you create your very own Web pages.

The order in which you choose to explore the projects is up to you. A good way to start is to skim the table of contents with your child and mark the titles that catch his or her interest. Read through the marked projects and choose one to try first.

Another way to approach the book is to connect a project to what your child is studying in school. The Internet is full of information to use in class assignments.

The Internet Is Always Growing

The Internet is dynamic, which means it is constantly changing and growing. What you find there today may be gone tomorrow.

So that you don't get stuck in any of the projects in this book, every project lists a variety of resources on the Internet. This way, if one address has changed or just plain disappeared from the Internet, there are many others to try.

Even with extensive checking and rechecking, some of the addresses listed in this book may not be valid any longer. Be patient and make sure to learn how to use the search tools described in Chapter 1. These tools will let you search the Internet for sites and information about the topics that interest your children.

This book offers a whole host of suggested sites on the Internet to visit, but it also includes strategies for searching the Internet for sites that are uniquely compelling to you and your children. This book does not assume that you use one specific tool for browsing the Web. That is, you will not find instructions for how to use browsers like Netscape Navigator and Microsoft's Internet Explorer. The strategies are presented so that regardless of what tool you use, your child can successfully complete the project.

Safety Is an Issue

We've all heard the horror stories in the media of kids stumbling upon sites with inappropriate content, or even being contacted directly by individuals with inappropriate intentions. These dangers are real. The

Internet is a public arena where a variety of opinions, behavior, and information exists. However, many parents have discovered several easy-to-implement strategies for protecting their children from these dangers:

★ Use only first names when posting notes and sending messages online and do not share addresses or telephone numbers with anyone.

★ You and your child are in control of where you go on the Internet, so if you don't like what you are seeing online, quit or exit from that site.

★ Respect the people on the Internet with whom you communicate. You can't see the people, but you are still responsible for what you say to them.

Keep in mind that there are both nice and not-so-nice people on the Internet, just as in the real world, and you may want to supervise what your kids are seeing online.

Filtering and Monitoring Software

Several different products protect your child as well as provide you with a review of where they go during a session on the Internet. Filtering software will actually block the child from entering a site that has content matching a predetermined list of inappropriate language. Monitoring software, sometimes included in filtering programs, can be helpful to use with slightly older kids because you are provided with a summary of their navigation without necessarily shutting doors to information.

One of the problems with these tools, particularly filtering software, is that the predetermined list does not take context into account. For instance, if a kid is doing a report on breast cancer, the software will restrict many sites because of the word "breast," even though it is not used in a porno-graphic context.

> **Several filtering and monitoring products are available, including Net Nanny** (http://www.netnanny.com)**, Cyber Patrol** (http://www.microsys.com/cyber/default.htm)**, and SurfWatch** (http://www.surfwatch.com)**.**

Appropriate Use Agreement

The idea of creating a written agreement with kids about appropriately using the Internet is actually borrowed from schools. Many schools across the country require students and, often the parents as well, to sign a contract stating that the student will only go to sites that contain appro-priate content. You can find many samples of different contracts on the Web. You may need to adapt what you find for home use, but the concept of developing agreed-upon ground rules is the same.

> **The Web 66 site (see Figure F.1) provides links to schools' Web sites and includes several links to sam-ple appropriate use documents:** http://mustang.coled .umn.edu/Started/use/Acceptableuse.html

Parental Supervision

Rather than depending on software tools as supervision replacement, you can always do the job of the software (and probably better) by working with your child during Internet sessions. If you approach this activity as a "parent who wants to learn" as opposed to a "parent who wants to check up on their kid," your child will probably be excited to include you in their explorations.

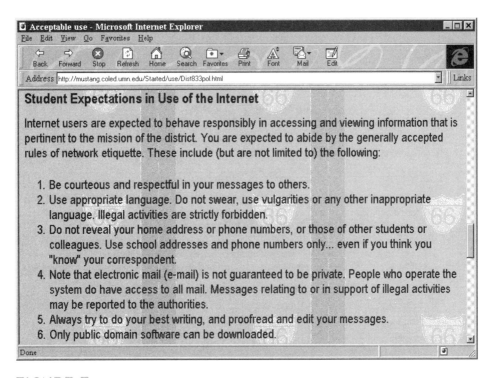

FIGURE F.1: **One school's Acceptable Use Policy**

Several Internet sites include information and ideas specifically for parents such as: ParentsPlace.com (http://www.parentsplace.com) shown in Figure F.2, the Librarians Guide to Cyberspace for Parents and Kids (http://wwww.ala.org/parents), Parents Guide to the Information Super Highway (http://wwww.childrenspartnership.org), and the Guide to Internet Parenting from Voters Telecommunications Watch (http://wwww.vtw.org/parents).

FIGURE F.2:   ParentsPlace.com

Capturing Software

Another strategy for providing Internet access to kids in a safe way with the help of a tool is to capture all aspects of a particular site and allow the child to explore those sites on your local desktop computer. By doing so, the child is not actually "online" while they are working with information and resources at a particular site. This strategy eliminates danger while still providing access. The difficulty with this strategy is that the sites must be captured first before the child can begin to explore.

 **NOTE**

An example of capturing software is Web-Wacker, available at most computer software stores.

Social Development

One common advantage often attributed to using the Internet is that everyone becomes equal because all the visual and nonverbal conversational cues are missing. This allows the young to speak to the old and the shy to speak to the bold in relative security and equality. Thus, kids can learn to discuss and debate with a wide array of people as they develop their communication skills.

Personal Development

The Internet opens access to a vast range of subjects, directions, and projects. Almost any whim or wonder can be pursued and discovered.

Open exploration that has the purpose of broadening background and understanding is valuable. All activity on the Internet does not have to be focused or intentional. It is good to reflect with kids on what they do and what they learn.

Cultural Development

Because of the easy access to people and information on the Internet, kids have great opportunities to discover things about themselves and others outside their cultures. Even if you live in an isolated community, you can learn about how others, both close and far, live their lives.

Because communication can be personal and relatively intimate, kids can find Net pals—like pen pals—and share much about themselves and their cultures.

Intellectual Development

The Internet brings worldwide resources, including information, ideas, issues, and people, to your computer. Using these resources can contribute much to success in school. Even more significant is the gradual vocabulary, conceptual, and organizational development that can occur. As with most important developmental influences, the real benefits accrue over time.

Empower the Kids

Put the computer and this book in the hands of kids and watch them go. When kids are at the helm of a project and decide where to go and what to see, they will be in control of their own learning. They will be empowered to chart their own course for what to learn next.

Watch and let your kids have successes and make errors. This is how they will learn; by trying things out on their own and by talking about what they did that worked and what failed. Be as willing to listen and discuss as you are to show and tell.

This book will help you both have fun and learn together using the Internet.

A Letter from Senator Bob Kerrey

Dear Parents:

The chapters that follow are not so much an instructional manual as a tour guide for an educational journey that will take you across the globe at the touch of a button. The Internet and telecommunications technology are changing our world in profound ways. The way we communicate, work, and learn is fundamentally different, and you must be prepared for it.

The Internet for Your Kids provides a wonderful start. The authors are to be commended for understanding and showing us that the Internet is a valuable educational tool that will help our kids learn today and for the rest of their lives.

If our children can master the skills laid out for them in the ensuing pages, the doors to opportunity will be thrown open. The currency of power and opportunity in the 21st Century will be information, and when it comes to information, the Internet is a gold mine.

There will never be a substitute, nor should there be, for the real fuel behind the American dream: ingenuity, hard work, and risk. But telecommunications technology—especially as embodied in the Internet—will help the engine of the American dream use that fuel in new and exciting ways. So I encourage everyone—parent, teacher, and child alike—who turns to the beginning of this book: learn the Internet and use this technology to the utmost. Dream. Learn. Explore. As *The Internet for Your Kids* shows, a whole new American frontier lies before us.

—Bob Kerrey

Bob Kerrey represents the state of Nebraska in the United States Senate.

The World of the Internet

If you could visit anywhere in the world, where would you go? France? South Africa? China? With your computer and its link to the Internet, you can now go to nearly any country, visit museums, parks, and libraries, and meet kids from all around the world. You are a traveler who has the world at your fingertips. Where would you like to start?

In this chapter, we'll talk about the equipment you need to start traveling the Internet. (If you already have an Internet connection and account set up, you can skip to the "Using the Internet" section to start learning about some tools of the Internet.) The Internet is a collection, or *network*, of computers around the globe that are linked together. With an Internet account, which gives you access to all these computers, you can travel across the network to find information or people. The Internet has been around for a long time and has been used by scientists, researchers, and university professors. It's also available to anyone who is interested in using it—like you!

Don't be intimidated by your computer or the technical terms of the Internet—just jump right in and you'll find them easy to use!

As you learn how to navigate through the maze of networks, you will discover that the Internet is like a giant connect-the-dots that surrounds the earth, only the dots are computers. As you explore the Internet, your computer is actually connecting to other computers all around the world to transfer information, help you visit people and places, and send and receive communications from anywhere and everywhere on the globe.

Because the computers are connected electronically, you can collect the best information from each and use it to help you achieve a goal. It's easy to tap into a variety of sources around the world quickly and easily to gather the information you're looking for. Maybe you want to find out when the next Bulls game is, find out about the making of a new movie, gather information about a recent hurricane, or get easy recipes so you can make dinner for your family. On the Internet you can find written information, pictures, sounds, and even digitized movies. No matter what you are interested in, the Internet can help. Some computers on the Internet also have *databases*, which are large collections of information that you can search.

This book has many different projects that will help you move from computer to computer, find and get the information you want, and have fun with the information once you've got it. There's a lot to choose from! Let your own personal interests guide you to the projects as you pick ones that sound fun or interesting to you.

The Internet is open 24 hours a day, so you can travel whenever you want. But before you jump on your computer, rev it up to warp speed, and dash around the Internet, check your equipment and read the directions for using the Internet tools explained in this chapter. You'll enjoy the projects in this book much more if you take the time to prepare yourself and your computer for the world of the Internet.

Your Ticket to the Internet

The most important piece of equipment you need for every activity is you. The Internet is made up of computers, networks, programs, and the people who use them. Your unique personality and interests will lead you to cross paths with people who are experts, people who have questions, people who share feelings, people who speak different languages… people like you!

To Make the Most of Your Adventure on the Internet:

- Use your imagination
- Prepare to explore new places
- Don't worry if you make a mistake—think of your mistakes as chances to learn something new
- Ask for help (and be sure to say "thanks!")
- Show people the same respect you would if they were sitting right next to you

Checking Your Equipment

Once you're ready, let's make sure you have the right equipment. Here's what you'll need:

- a personal computer of any kind

- communications software (often this comes with a computer or is provided when you sign up for an online service; if not, it's available from your local computer store)

- a modem (recommended speed: 28,800 bits per second or faster)

- a connection to your phone line

If you aren't already set up for this, you'll need to ask your parents or another adult for help. They can speak with a representative of the local computer store and find out what additional equipment or software you may need. Be patient! It may take some time to get it working, but it is well worth the wait.

If someone telephones while you're *online* (or when your modem is plugged into the tele- phone jack and you are connected to the Internet), they will hear a busy signal. You are already on the line, just as if you were mak- ing a regular phone call. If you have Call Waiting, you may get cut off from the Internet if your phone line rings. Check with your local phone company to find out how you can tem- porarily turn off your Call Waiting while you're online.

Getting an Internet Account

You have now checked your equipment and have a road map (this book), but you still need a ticket to get through the Internet tollbooth. The ticket is actually your own personal address on the Internet that you will use to get on and off the network. This address will be yours. No one else can use it, because you will also have a secret password.

To get an address and password, you have to establish an Internet account through a commercial network, a state network, a local univer- sity, or a private company. Check with your parents or teacher to see whether you already have access to an Internet account. If you don't, ask someone who is already online if you can use their computer. Point their Web browser at `http://www.tagonline.com/Providers/` to get a cur- rent list of Internet service providers.

A *Web browser* is software that lets you get to thousands of interesting sites on the Internet. (See the glossary in Appendix B for definitions of terms you may not know.) We'll read more about Web browsers later in this chapter in "World Wide Web."

With an Internet Account You Can:

- Publish your own story in an online magazine

- Play games like Scrabble or Chess with people on the other side of the world

- Join forces with kids all over the world to conduct scientific experiments

- Become a character in an online adventure game

- Create your own personal Web page so that people can visit your Web site

When calling a company about Internet accounts, there are several questions to be sure to ask:

★ What is the price for setting up a basic account with Internet access?

★ What services does a basic account include?

★ What is the price to keep the Internet account? (There is usually a fee you pay every month.)

★ Is there a local phone number to access the account, or do you have to call long-distance?

★ Does the company provide a user manual?

Using the Internet

The activities in this book direct you toward many different places and resources on the Internet that let you do many different things.

Internet accounts come with features that let you explore a variety of collections, sites, and activities. You can also meet and exchange ideas with people through e-mail, chat groups, newsgroups, and online games. Here is a list of several Internet tools and how you can use them:

Electronic mail (also called *e-mail*)	You can send and receive messages from friends around the world
Web browsing	You can access information by clicking on highlighted or underlined text or icons that are linked to other documents in other places
Listservs (also called *mailing lists*)	You can be part of a number of people (a list) who receive information on a certain topic
Gopher	You can look at information organized by this menu-based system
Telnet	You can operate other computers around the world from your computer after connecting through the Internet
Usenet newsgroups	You can see what others say and post your own messages in conferences, forums, or discussions concerning a specific topic
IRC (Internet Relay Chat)	You can have real-time online discussions in this area of the Internet
MUD (multi-user dungeon) or MUSE (multi-user simulated environment)	You can create a character and participate in online role-playing games in this area of the Internet

People use two major Internet tools to find what they need and to communicate with others—electronic mail (e-mail) and the World Wide Web (WWW). We'll explore each of these in turn.

Electronic Mail (E-Mail)

I've got mail!

Through the Internet, you can exchange messages electronically with people all over the world. All day and all night, messages speed back and forth. The cost is always less than a long-distance phone call and much faster than "snail mail," or mail that travels through the postal service. For instance, let's say you live in Mankato, Minnesota, and you want to send a letter to a friend who lives in London, England. The letter may take almost a week to reach your friend if you send it through the post office, but if you send an e-mail, the message could reach your friend within minutes. Of course, you and your friend each must have some sort of *e-mail program*.

You can choose from many different e-mail programs. The most popular commercial program currently in use today is called Eudora (pronounced "you-dora"). You can find out more information and download a copy at http://www.qualcomm.com. A Web site such as HotMail offers free e-mail to subscribers. Take a look at their Web site at http://www.hotmail.com. (For more information about downloading, see "The World of Communications Software" later in this chapter.)

All e-mail programs include similar features but may use slightly different names and commands. For example, the procedure to see what e-mail other people have sent you might be called "Check Messages" in one e-mail program, and "Get Mail" in another. Most products have a Help button you can click on to get information about how to use the program.

E-mail messages are made up of two main parts: the header and the body. The header contains all the addressing information, just like the front of an envelope, while the body contains the actual message. Let's take a look at each item, one at a time. Check out Figure 1.1 to see what an e-mail message looks like.

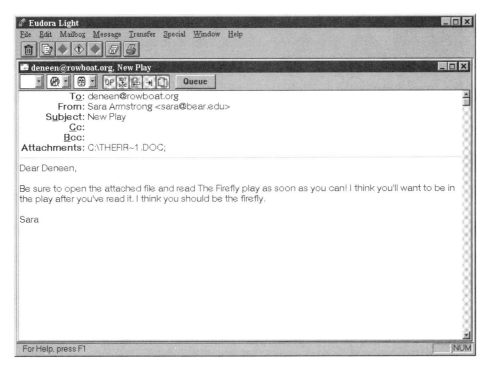

FIGURE 1.1: This is an example of an e-mail message sent using the e-mail program Eudora.

To:

When you send any e-mail message, you'll want to make sure that the To section is filled in accurately, or the message may not be received. An address might look like this: `deneen@rowboat.org`. The first part, `deneen`, is a user name. It's the name of a person, or the name a person has given to his or her account. Everything after the @ identifies the computer that houses that person's account. (The symbol @ is called the "at sign," so you would substitute the word "at" in its place when you read the address aloud.) The last three letters refer to the type of organization the computer belongs. For example, `org` means the computer is connected to the Internet through an organization service.

Six main endings show the types of organizations where people have their Internet accounts:

com	commercial organizations
edu	educational organizations
gov	governmental organizations
mil	military organizations
org	other organizations
net	network resource organizations

Notice that there are no spaces between any of the parts of an Internet address and that some parts are separated by periods. When you give your Internet address to someone else, you'll read the period as "dot." For example, we can pretend that my Internet address is deneen@rowboat.org, which would be pronounced "deneen at rowboat dot org."

Why don't you now try giving your e-mail address to a friend, pronouncing it with these guidelines?

From:

When you first set up your e-mail software, you'll be asked to put in your e-mail address, which will then automatically appear on every message you write. In fact, most e-mail programs insert your e-mail address, along with your name, so that when other people get your messages, they have an idea who the messages are from before opening them. The From line might look like this:

```
saarmst@bear.edu (Sara Armstrong)
```

or

```
Sara Armstrong <saarmst@bear.edu>
```

Subject:

The Subject line is like a headline for your message—a brief phrase to say what your message is about. You will want to be as specific as you can in a few words so that the person receiving your message will pay attention to your message and want to read it right away. For example, if you are asking someone if you can quote them in a report you are doing, you might type "Permission Request" in the Subject line. Many e-mail programs also let you indicate the priority of your message—such as lowest, low, normal, high, highest. This priority will tell the person how important your message is.

Cc: and Bcc:

Cc is short for *carbon copy*. If someone's e-mail address is shown there, it means that he or she also got a copy of the message.

Bcc stands for *blind carbon copy*. There may be a time when you want to send a copy of a message to someone, without the person listed in the To section knowing about it. In that case, type the e-mail address for the copy in the Bcc space, and it won't show up in the message header when the person listed in the To section gets the message.

Attachments:

It's pretty easy to send a picture, sound, or text file to a friend with an e-mail message. In your e-mail program, you'll find a button or pull-down menu item that says "Attachment" or "Attach a File." When you click on that button or highlight the phrase, you will be asked to find and open the file you want to attach, just as you would open a file in a word processing document. When your message is received, the person you've sent it to will see the name of the file you've attached and will be able to open the file. Sometimes you need special software to open an attachment. Refer to your e-mail software manual or Help pages to find out any special tricks or hints you can use to be most successful at sending and receiving attachments.

Message Text

This is called the *body* of the message, and it's where you type what you want to say. Some e-mail programs limit the length of the message, but there is usually plenty of space to create complete and detailed messages.

If your message is an answer to someone's question (called a *reply*), be sure you say this at the beginning of your message. Often, your mail program will have a Reply button that automatically addresses your message. Make sure the person you're replying to has all the information needed to understand your reply. You may want to include the question in the message that you're replying to. For example, let's say a friend sends you a message asking, "How are you? Did you watch the Oscars last night?" If you reply to this message and say, "Great! No, I missed them," your friend may not know what you're talking about. She may have sent out several different messages to different people asking different questions. Instead, you can include her text in the body of your message, like this:

```
>> How are you?

Great!

>> Did you watch the Oscars last night?

No, I missed them.
```

Now that you know the basics of e-mail, try sending a friend an e-mail message and then replying to the message that you get back. Remember, you'll have to know your friend's e-mail address.

Other E-Mail Features

Once you know some friends' e-mail addresses, you can build an address file of people whose e-mail addresses you would like to have on hand, very much like an address book where you write in your friends' names, addresses, and phone numbers. The people in your electronic address book will usually be people you plan to send e-mail to on a regular basis. Check your e-mail software to find out exactly how to create, add to, and delete the address book file.

Sometimes when you receive an e-mail message, you will see something at the end—it could be a picture made with keyboard characters, or an interesting saying, or more information about the person who wrote the message. Figure 1.2 shows an example.

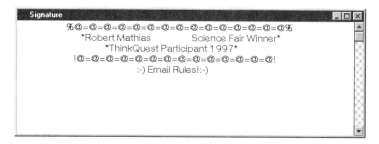

FIGURE 1.2: **You can create a signature as fun as this one!**

This is called a *sig file* (which stands for *signature file*), and most e-mail programs let you create one. Once you make a sig file, it will be automatically included in every message you send. Often sig files include the writer's name and contact information. Be sure you do not include any personal information, such as your home phone number or address.

It's not a good idea to send out personal information unless your parents say it's OK. Communicating with people you haven't met in person on the Internet can lead to good, solid friendships, but occasionally, it's better to play it safe with your contact information and not include it.

Your e-mail program also will probably let you send a single message to a group of people at the same time so that you don't have to type and send the same message over and over again to several different people. This feature is called a *nickname*, and it's pretty simple to use. First, you decide on a word or name that will remind you of the group of people you are putting together. For example, if you are organizing a soccer team, and you have to get in touch with the members on a regular basis, you might give the nickname "Soccer" to the list of members that includes the e-mail addresses of everyone in the group. Then, you type in the e-mail addresses of everyone you want to include in the group. From then on, every time you want to send a message to all those people, you just type **Soccer** in the To space, and the message will go to everyone in the group.

When you use nicknames, or send messages to a lot of people, you want to be sure that the messages will be ones people want to get. A few years ago, some lawyers got in trouble by sending an unwanted advertisement to a lot of people on the Internet. Their unwanted action is called *spamming*, and it makes a lot of people angry because their mailboxes get full. In fact, service providers sometimes terminate the accounts of people who spam others. If you receive a number of unwanted messages, you can contact your service provider, who will put a stop to it.

A Final Word on E-Mail

Most e-mail programs will automatically include your e-mail address in the message you are sending. This is helpful because then you do not have to type in your address (like the return address on a regular letter) every time you send a new message.

E-mail is your personal connection to the Internet, which you can use to send messages to just one other person or to a group of people. Check your e-mail instructions to find out how to set up your address book and group mail. You can make friends quickly on the Internet, and you may begin to receive many messages every day to which you can respond quickly and easily using your e-mail features. Now we'll talk about the other common use of the Internet—the World Wide Web (WWW).

World Wide Web (WWW)

In the last several years, a new kind of software has been developed that makes it easy and exciting to get to all kinds of places online. The software is called a *browser*, and it allows us to navigate the World Wide Web (also called WWW, or the Web). The Web is the part of the Internet where documents and images from people all over the world are linked together. Individuals, companies, and organizations can all have a presence on the Web, called a *Web site*. Web browsers provide a graphical interface (GUI—pronounced "goo-ey") between you and the sites. (A *graphical user interface* uses pictures and icons, rather than just words to display the Web sites. There are more Web sites today than we can count—and all are different from each other and constantly changing.) Figure 1.3 shows Navigator 4, a graphical Web browser made by Netscape, at the Discovery Channel's Web site. By moving your mouse and clicking on pictures, icons, and words, you will be able to travel to unexpected and exciting places.

The World Wide Web is NOT linear...

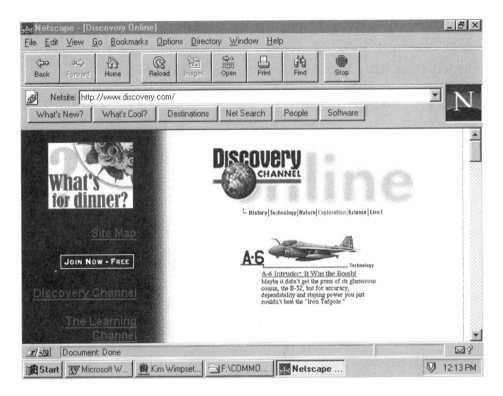

FIGURE 1.3: **The Navigator browser lets you surf the Web.**

The Web is not linear. That means that it's different from turning pages in a certain order like in a book. Because of *hypertext links,* or connections between sites, you may start out on a music site, travel to a particular musician's *home page*, and end up at a site in France because the artist will be performing there soon. (A home page is a main Web page designed to provide information about a particular person, organization, or place—in this case, the musician you came across at the music site.) From there, you might link to a page where you can learn French, or see the French flag amid others at a site that has a collection of flags from around the world. Because you might get interested in visiting a number of places you hadn't planned to visit when you were using the Internet, be sure you understand the time limits your parents or teacher have in mind for your Internet explorations.

Web sites use hypertext links (text that is highlighted, underlined, and/or a color other than black; also called *links*) to connect different sections, or pages, on a single computer, or on computers all around the world. For example, the Melrose School Web site includes stories and drawings by students at the school, which you get to by clicking on hypertext links (see Figure 1.4). Melrose School, part of the Oakland Unified School District in Oakland, California, has a Web page on the District's site. From that page (see Figure 1.5), you can link to other schools in the district, as well as other Web resources from around the world.

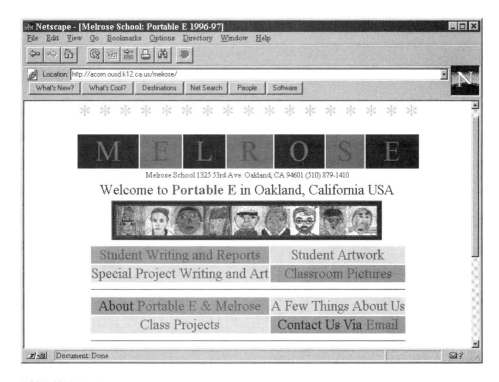

At the Melrose School Web site you can check out stories and art from students.

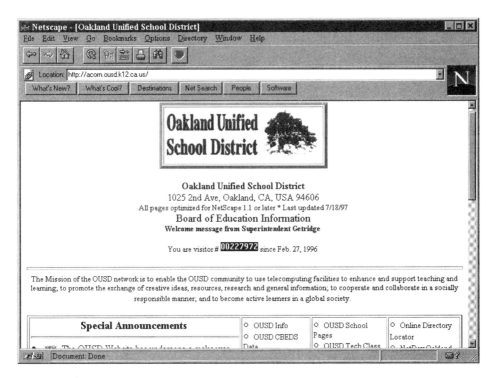

The Oakland Unified School District Web site provides links to district schools, as well as resources for students, teachers, and the community.

You may be wondering how to find such Web sites as the Melrose School Web site and the Oakland Unified School District Web site. Each Web page has a distinct address on the Web. If you know the address for a Web site, all you have to do is type it into your Web browser and then your Web browser will take you there! Web addresses, or URLs (uniform resource locators), are made up of several parts. They all begin in the same way: http://.

http stands for *hypertext transfer protocol*, and refers to the method all Web programmers use to identify their sites and links. Then comes the particular address of the site. Web addresses often start with www (for World Wide Web), but they don't have to. As in e-mail addresses, the parts of the Web address refer to the computer where the site is housed. The last part of the address may be .com, .edu, .gov, .mil, .net, or .org, just like e-mail. You might also find an address that ends in a country abbreviation, such as .us, or .br (United States or Brazil). Some K-12 school addresses include this information in their address. You might find an address that ends in k12.ca.us, or k12.ak.us, for schools or school districts in California or Alaska.

It is very important to type a Web address *exactly* as it appears. Type uppercase and lowercase letters where they belong, with no spaces, and all the dots and slashes in the right places, and so on. If even one character is incorrect, you will get a message indicating that there is no such place, or it couldn't be found. If you get this message, double-check the address before moving onto a different site.

The most common Web browsers are Netscape Navigator, which can be found at http://www.netscape.com, and Microsoft Internet Explorer, which you will find at http://www.microsoft.com. If you don't have a Web browser, go to your local library or ask to use a friend's computer. Use their browser to go to these addresses and get a browser of your own. You will see that these browsers have some features that are similar to your word processor, such as Save As and Print. They also have some special features that let you collect sites, find your way back to a site you visited earlier, and search for specific information you need.

Bookmarks or Favorites

Suppose you come across a wonderful site that has the most fabulous dinosaur collection you've ever seen (you may want to check out the

University of California's Museum of Paleontology at `http://ucmp1`
`.berkeley.edu`), but you don't want to have to write down the address,
or type it in every time you want to visit. Not to worry! Depending on the
Web browser you are using, you simply pull down a menu item and highlight Add a Bookmark or Add Page to Favorites (see Figure 1.6). The next
time you come to the computer and want to visit that Web site, go to the
bookmark or favorites menu item, pull down the file, and highlight
Museum of Paleontology. You'll immediately be connected there. The
computer keeps the address for the museum in its memory so you don't
have to!

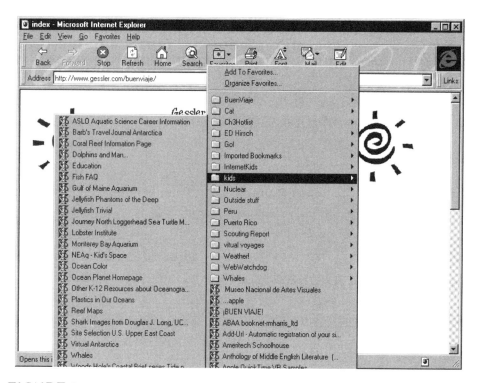

FIGURE 1.6: **Internet Explorer's Favorites listing keeps Web
addresses so that you don't have to.**

During an online session, you may decide you'd like to return to a site you visited earlier. For example, by pulling down a menu in Navigator called Go (see Figure 1.7), you can highlight the earlier site and you'll be taken there. Instead of having to bookmark all of the sites you've visited, or write down addresses, your browser software takes care of the record-keeping for you. However, the Go feature only tracks the sites you've visited during your online session. When you log off, the Go list disappears, and a new one will begin when you log on the next time.

Back takes you back one page
Forward takes you forward one page
Print prints the current page

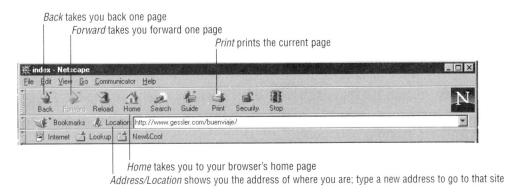

Home takes you to your browser's home page
Address/Location shows you the address of where you are; type a new address to go to that site

FIGURE 1.7: **Pull down Netscape Navigator's Go menu to revisit your online session's sites.**

Searching the Web

Some people say that locating something on the Internet is like trying to find a particular book in a library where all the books have been dumped into a pile. You know the book is there, but you're not sure how to find it. On the Internet, a number of search tools have been developed to help you find what you're looking for. Generally, they fall into two categories: *search engines* and *directories*, which refer to how the tool searches for information on the Internet. Yahoo! is an example of a search directory, and AltaVista is an example of a search engine. All these tools can be found by pressing the Net Search or Search button on your browser. You'll be taken to a page with links to a number of tools. You'll probably want to experiment with several until you find two or three that seem to work best for you. See also *Search Tools*.

Search engines are easy to use. Usually you type in a keyword or words that you are looking for, and the engine matches up what you're looking for with sites from around the world. It makes its best "guess" as to which sites match what you want, and you'll see a list, with links to the pages. If you see a page that seems hopeful, click on the link and find out. If not, go back to the search results and try a few others. If none of them seem to work, you'll want to change the words, usually by getting more specific. You will also find that every search tool provides information on its page as to how to perform an advanced search, as well as help with using the tool most effectively.

TIP

When you're searching for something, try enclosing the words in quotation marks so the search tool will only identify pages with the words together. For example, type **"Disney movies"** rather than **Disney movies**. Without the quotes, the search tool will look for all the pages that have either "Disney" or "movies" on them. With the quotes, the engine will only list pages with the actual phrase "Disney movies."

Sometimes you can find the page you're looking for by removing the end section (or sections) of a long Web address. For example, if there was a site with the address `http://www.games.com/adventure/exploration/Africa/wild.animals` and you got a message saying "Site not found," you could try re-entering the address without `wild.animals`. If that didn't work, you could try removing `Africa/`, and so on. Eventually, if you got all the way back to `www.games.com`, you might see options at the site that you could click on to find exactly what you were looking for.

Search Tools

You can use the following search tools to help you find exactly what you're looking for:

Yahooligans!	http://www.yahooligans.com
Yahoo!	http://www.yahoo.com
Excite	http://www.excite.com
Altavista	http://www.altavista.digital.com
Hotbot	http://www.hotbot.com
Infoseek	http://www.infoseek.com
Magellan	http://www.mckinley.com
Lycos	http://www.lycos.com
WebCrawler	http://www.webcrawler.com

Directory search tools set up categories from which you can choose so that you can narrow your search from the beginning. For example, if you are interested in finding information in sports, recreation, education, or other categories, you might try this kind of search tool. Yahoo! is a good example of a directory tool. A special site, Yahooligans! (http://www .yahooligans.com), has been designed especially for kids. Check it out!

Giving Credit Where Credit Is Due

Everything on the Web was created by somebody. This means that if you copy information, pictures, graphics, sounds, movies, or any other data, and use that information, you *must* credit the person and Web site. Just as you want credit for your own work, you will want to offer the same respect to others. There are even sites online that tell you how, exactly, to give credit. You might want to take a look at Purdue University's Writing Lab at http://owl.trc.purdue.edu/files/110.html.

Now that you know how to send an e-mail to a friend and explore the Web, you're on your way to mastering the Internet. Although e-mail and the Web are the two most common uses of the Internet, there are many other features to check out as well. We'll learn about listservs next.

Listservs (Mailing Lists)

Mailing lists (which are called *listservs*—short for "mailing list servers") allow e-mail to be sent to a group of people interested in a particular topic. For example, you might join a listserv that keeps you updated about space flights or discussions about the latest movies. When anyone in the group *posts* (or sends) a message to the listserv, you can send a message back to just that person or to the entire listserv.

To subscribe (or join) to a listserv, you must first send a message to the computer that has the listserv. When you subscribe, you will need to include two important pieces of information: the name of the listserv and the address of the listserv. For example, to subscribe to a listserv called Kidzmail at the computer address asuvm.inre.asu.edu, you would send an e-mail message to the address listserv@asuvm.inre.asu.edu. Leave the subject line blank and type only the word **subscribe** followed by the name of the listserv, followed by your full name (not your Internet account name). Note that each of these is separated by one space. Figure 1.8 shows an e-mail message that will subscribe Sara Armstrong to the listserv call Kidlink (this message was sent using Eudora). As you can tell from the list's name, kids who subscribe will be talking about their interests and issues. To find more, see *Getting a List of Listservs*

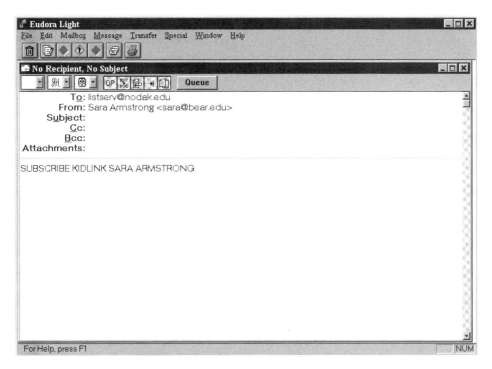

FIGURE 1.8: **When you want to subscribe to a listserv, send an e-mail message similar to this one.**

Getting a List of Listservs

There are several lists of operating listservs, which cover a wide range of topics, available through the Internet. These are very long files and will take a long time to get into your computer. Two examples on the Web are:

```
http://www.cuc.edu/cg.pli-bin/listservform
http://www.nova.edu/Inter-Links/listserv/listhlp.html
```

You can usually tell what people who belong to a listserv will be writing messages about by the name of the listserv. For example, in the

Kidzmail listserv, kids are writing about their interests. There are so many listservs that you can find one for just about anything you like to talk about: movies, sports, you name it. You will also find many lists in this book that you can join, and they're all free!

NOTE

Watch out! If you subscribe to too many list-servs, you may receive hundreds of messages a day and not have time to read them all. Be selective, and if you get flooded with too much mail, unsubscribe. To unsubscribe, follow the directions for subscribing but replace the word "subscribe" in the message area with "unsubscribe."

The following tools of the Internet are less commonly used than e-mail, the Web, and listservs, but they're also a great way to travel the world on your computer. We'll talk about Gopher next.

Gopher

Some computers on the Internet contain text articles and files with no pictures or links about all sorts of topics. To find these computers, you can use a computer program called Gopher that was created at the University of Minnesota, home of the "Golden Gophers." Just like the real rodent that tunnels through the ground, the program tunnels through the Internet to point out articles that you can bring into your own computer. Gopher is easy to use because it has text-based menus of choices at every step. You can select the item you want, which may take you to another list, and eventually the file you want. For an example, check out the Gopher menu shown in Figure 1.9. Each computer that uses the Gopher software is called a *Gopher server*, and all these Gophers together do their work in *Gopherspace*. You can get to Gopher servers through your Web browser. Instead of typing **http://** at the beginning of the address, you will type **gopher://** and then the rest of the address.

Another feature of the Internet that allows you to connect to another computer is Telnet. We'll talk about this next.

Great Gopher Sites

Education Gopher at Florida Tech
gopher://sci-ed.fit.edu

Searchable Film Database
gopher://hugo.lib.ryrson.ca:70/
11gopher_root%3A5Bsubjects
.audio_visual.watmedia%5D

Professional Sports Schedules
gopher://gopher.bsu.edu

```
Netscape - [gopher://sci-ed.fit.edu/]
File  Edit  View  Go  Bookmarks  Options  Directory  Window  Help

Location: gopher://sci-ed.fit.edu/

What's New?   What's Cool?   Destinations   Net Search   People   Software
```

Gopher Menu

- Welcome to the Florida Tech Education Gopher
- Search All Menus on this Server
- Education
- Electronic Texts
- Internet
- Libraries
- Reference Desk (Dict., Thesaurus, zip/area codes)
- Search Tools (Archie, Veronica, etc.)
- Selected FTP Sites
- Selected Gophers and Information Servers
- Subject Area Resources
- University Information Services

```
gopher://winnie.fit.edu:70/11/subj
```

FIGURE 1.9: **From the Education Gopher at Florida Tech, you have access to a number of reference tools.**

Telnet (Remote Log-In)

Telnet is a feature of the Internet that allows you to connect directly to another computer on the Internet and operate this computer from your own computer. Just as you log into a system to use e-mail or get information through a Gopher, you use Telnet to go to a totally different computer and explore or even get an account there.

To use Telnet, you will need special software that you can obtain by pointing your Web browser to `http://tucows.phoenix.net` and then selecting the type of computer you're using. When you select Telnet, you'll be provided with several Telnet software options. From there, follow the directions for installation.

When using Telnet, you'll also need to know the specific Internet address of a computer with information you would like to explore. The address will look just like the part of your own personal address that comes after the @ symbol. For example, the Telnet address for the Global Land Information site is `glis.cr.usgs.gov` where you can get geographical information about anyplace in the world.

Now you are ready to go. Because each computer you will telnet to will be a little different, it is important to read the information that appears when you first connect to the other computer.

When you use Telnet, the initial screen will usually have directions explaining the commands you will need to use to move around the computer, special policies or rules you must respect for continued use of the computer, and a description of what files and programs are available to you. Figure 1.10 shows the University of Michigan's Weather Underground site.

In case you get stuck somewhere and want to get out, learn an emergency exit command (one that will get you back to your host network). One emergency exit command is "ctrl-]". This means you press the control (Ctrl) key and hold it while typing] (the right bracket). If you're using a computer at school, you may want to ask someone who answers technical questions on your network (your network administrator) to suggest an emergency exit command before you telnet to another computer. Check out *Great Telnet Sites*.

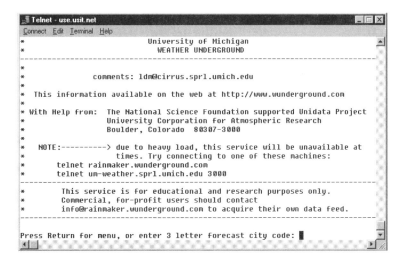

FIGURE 1.10: **At the University of Michigan's Weather Underground site, you can find out about weather patterns and other information.**

Great Telnet Sites

NASA Spacelink	**Telnet to** spacelink.msfc.nasa.gov **no login required**
National Weather Service	**Telnet to** esdim1.nodc.noaaa.gov **login: guest**
Global Land information	**Telnet to** glis.cr.usgs.gov **login: guest**
National Weather Forecasts	**Telnet to** downwind.sprl.umich.edu **no login required**

Usenet Newsgroups

Newsgroups are also called *conferences*. There are thousands of different newsgroups covering many topics, from television shows to politics to chess. In newsgroups, anyone can leave a message, read a message, or respond to a message. These newsgroups run on a network called Usenet, which is part of the Internet. They're like mailing lists where you can read a lot of different messages from people, but instead of messages getting mailed to you, in a newsgroup you go to an area to read messages.

Usenet is made up of nine categories of newsgroups:

comp	Computer
news	News server software and networks
rec	Hobbies and recreational activities
sci	Scientific research
soc	Social issues
talk	Debate on controversial topics
humanities	Literature/fine arts
misc	Everything else
alt	Alternative

In most newsgroups (except those in the category alt), a moderator makes sure the messages are current, that people are being reasonably polite to each other, and that the topic is still interesting. To access Usenet groups, you will need newsreader software that you can usually get through your Internet service provider.

Middle school students discuss what's on their minds in the Usenet newsgroup called `k12.chat.junior` (see Figure 1.11). People talk about current and historical events in `soc.history`. These are only two groups chosen as examples from a list of more than 4,000 groups. See *Popular Usenet Groups* to find more. (By the way, alternative newsgroup—those groups that end with `alt`—are not supervised, and people post all kinds of notes that sometimes are not appropriate or respectful. Because of this, not all of the `alt` newsgroups are available at every Usenet site. Even though the network where you have your account decides which Usenet groups to offer to users, you're sure to find something that interests you.)

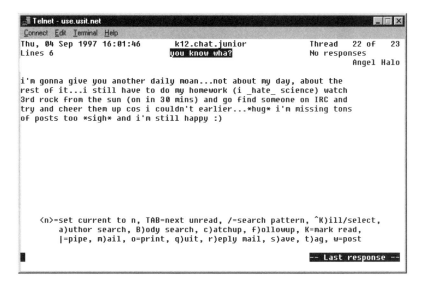

FIGURE 1.11: **This Usenet group offers opportunities for kids in middle school to talk to each other about a variety of topics.**

Popular Usenet Groups

`rec.arts.movies.current.films`	**People share their reviews of current movies**
`alt.irc`	**Kids participate in online chats**
`sci.astro.research`	**Kids talk about the latest in astronomical discoveries**

Internet Relay Chat (IRC)

Internet Relay Chat (IRC) offers an interesting way of using the Internet. People who are online at the same time can send messages to each other and read them instantly, as if they were "chatting" on the telephone.

IRC is called a *multi-user system*, which means that several people come online to groups (called *channels*). The channels are usually devoted to a specific topic of conversation, such as a recent space shuttle launch, school projects, or sporting events. It's a kind of online party with different *rooms* for different topics of conversation. See *Kidlink IRC* to check one out.

Kidlink IRC

Subscribe to the Kidlink listserv by sending e-mail to `list-servr@nodak.edu`. (Follow the instructions for subscribing to a listserv earlier in this chapter.) This listserv has its own private IRC for kids only.

You can get to IRC in two ways. Using Telnet, you can connect with another computer that is running a public IRC client, or you can have your own client on your computer. To find out how to get your own client—which is a more reliable method of using IRC—read the Usenet newsgroup `alt.irc`, where you can learn more about IRC.

Once you get into IRC, you will need to join a channel to chat with other people. Here are three IRC commands that will help you get started:

`/list<enter>`	gives you a list of all of the active channels
`/channel#<channel name>`	gives you access to a particular channel
`/quit<enter>`	gets you out of IRC

IRC tutorials provide many more commands that you can learn to move around the system and talk to more people.

Multi-User Dungeon (MUD) and Multi-User Simulated Environment (MUSE)

In a MUD or MUSE you participate in a game where you become another character and play that character's role in the environment you find yourself in. MUDs and MUSEs are similar to IRCs in that you will be interacting with people immediately rather than just leaving messages. When people log into a MUD or a MUSE, they become participants in a game or simulation. Similar to the game

Dungeons and Dragons, some MUDs and MUSEs are modeled after fantastical stories where the characters live in a world described in a book. Others are focused on interaction between the users in a chat mode, rather than playing parts in a story.

Great MUDs and MUSEs

TrekMUSE   Go to `telnet://trekmuse.org:1701`. **This MUSE is an educational muse with a space theme.**

MicroMUSE   **Point your Web browser to** `telnet://michael.ai.mit.edu`—**and login as guest. It's a vision of the 24th century—high tech with a social conscience.**

Each MUD or MUSE has a set of commands all its own, which makes learning how to move around and interact in a MUD or MUSE a challenge. Fortunately, there are sites for beginners where you can start your adventure. As you become a more experienced player, you can explore other MUDs and MUSEs that you find interesting.

There are many different names for multi-user environments on the Internet. In addition to MUDs, there are MOOs, MUSHes, MUSE-MUDs, and others. Each of these usually has a particular personality. For instance, DIKU-MUD usually involves a combat game. MUSE-MUDs are focused on social interaction.

Netiquette

When you start exploring the Internet, you will find that you are in contact with people you've never met in person. You will probably make new friends and work on a number of projects with kids in other countries.

People who do a lot of work on the Internet have found that it is important to pay more attention than usual to the words they are using in their messages. The reason for this concern is that when we are talking with someone face to face, we can tell a lot from their expressions and body language, such as whether they are interested, or if they understand when we're joking and not trying to make them mad. It's hard to be sure about these things when you can't see someone's face, or even hear their voice.

We're all interested in making sure other people understand what we are trying to say and do. People who use the Internet have developed some ways of writing online that helps make sure they're not offending anyone. *Etiquette* refers to the practices we follow to be polite offline; *netiquette* refers to such practices when we're online. For example, when you're writing an e-mail message or participating in a chat or newsgroup, do not write the whole message in capital letters. Some people say it looks like you're shouting. If you want to emphasize something, you can put asterisks (*) on either side of the word or words you want people to pay attention to. You might write, "It was *great* to see you yesterday!"

Another online custom is the use of *smileys*— little faces you can see if you look sideways at the screen, that show feelings. (See *Commonly Used Smileys*.)

Commonly Used Smileys

:-)	smiling face
:-(	frowning face
(-:	left-handed smiling face
%-)	smiling face with glasses
;-)	winking face
:-D	laughing face

People also often use initials to stand for words, such as abbreviations that are used as codes between friends. There are a number of these abbreviations that a lot of people understand. You can also make up your own for your messages, which only you and your friends will be able to figure out. (See *Commonly Used Abbreviations*.)

Commonly Used Abbreviations

F2F or FTF	face to face
RL	real life
BTW	by the way
IMHO	in my humble opinion
FOFL	falling on the floor laughing
BG	big grin
LOL	laughing out loud
TTFN	ta ta for now

Again, you probably have already thought of a *lot* of abbreviations you can use in your own messages!

Sometimes people get upset by a message or comment they receive, and instead of checking to see what the person was really trying to say, they respond with insults. This is called *flaming*, and if the original writer gets mad and sends more insults back, a *flame war* has begun. Sometimes it helps to remember that it's harder to make sure the other person understands what you're trying to say in an online message than in a phone call or in person, especially if you like to use sarcasm or teasing words. Be sure to re-read your message before you send it to make sure as best you can that your words will not be taken in the wrong way.

One place people can unintentionally annoy others is when they jump into a newsgroup or chat discussion without really understanding what it's about. If you're new to a group—a *newbie*—it's often a good idea to read the FAQ (frequently asked questions) file to find out what has already been explained. You also might want to *lurk*—read what others have written for awhile, before adding your comments.

Creating Your Own Internet Presence

There are a number of ways you can share your ideas and work with others worldwide. You can post your writing, art, and music to a number of sites, such as International Kids' Space (`http://www.kids-space.org`). You can participate in projects or contests such as ThinkQuest (`http://www.advanced.org/thinkquest`). Or you can create your own Web pages just for the fun of it. To do so, you need to know a little about the language in which Web pages are written. It's called HTML, or Hypertext Markup Language. You can find out all about it, and how to make great pages, from Web sites such as Beginner's Guide to HTML (`http://www.gnn.com/gnn/wic/html.03.html`) or Servo's Guide to Basic HTML (`http://www2.dockingbay.com/servo/HTML`). We'll talk more about HTML in Chapter 9.

Some people prefer to use Web editors, which offer graphical workspaces in which you can put text, pictures, charts, sounds, and other elements. Good, easy-to-use Web editors include Web Workshop, Claris HomePage, PageMill, FrontPage, and others. Check with friends, ask questions online, and try out a few. You'll soon find what tools best match your style. And you'll have plenty of opportunity to practice your skills with projects in this book. Remember, the Web is a place where you can really feel a part of the worldwide community.

The World of Communications Software

You will probably want to do several activities that are entirely separate from the Internet. These actions, like printing, are done with your communications software. You can use many different commercial or shareware programs, each of which will have its own ways of doing things. Be sure to read the instruction manual that comes with the software to learn about all of the commands. (*Shareware* programs are made available to you so you can try them out before you buy them. If you like them, follow the instructions in the program, and send the developer what he or she asks for: postcard, money, and so on).

When you are just learning to use telecommunications software and the Internet, it is difficult to figure out where the worlds of the Internet and your own computer begin and end. There are times when you may ask yourself, "Am I on the Internet right now?" If your modem is in use, and you are moving from your network to another computer by using telnet, FTP, Gopher, WWW, or IRC, you are on the Internet.

Uploading and Downloading

When you want to take a file from your computer and put it up on the Internet, it's called *uploading*. When you want to get a file from the Internet and bring it into your computer, it's called *downloading*.

To download something, you can often click on a picture, and you'll get an option to Save As. By naming the picture and indicating where you want it saved, you can look at if later when you've logged off.

You can also download trial programs of software by going to the company's Web site and following the instructions. Again, you'll designate where you want the program stored on your hard drive, so you can find it again.

Both uploading and downloading are done with your communications software. You can find out more about uploading and downloading by reading your instruction manual or asking someone who already knows how to do these procedures.

You will want to have a virus checker installed on your computer so that you can make sure automatically that all the files you download from the Internet are clean. (*Viruses* are programs that can wreak havoc on your computer and files.) E-mail messages and text files cannot carry viruses, but other programs can. You can check out two popular virus checkers and download trial versions at the following addresses: McAfee's VirusScan (http://www.mcafee.com) or Norton Anti-Virus (http://www.norton.com).

Printing

There are many different word processing and communications software packages, and the directions for printing and other commands are different for each. (This is also true for uploading, downloading, and logging on and off.) There are a lot of places to get help with all of these procedures. Check with your parents or teacher to find out where to go for help.

You're on Your Way!

The best way to learn is to try. As the saying goes, "If at first you don't succeed, try, try again!" If you can't get to a site you want, or don't get an answer to your e-mail message right away, don't worry. Just visit somewhere else, or start another project. If you have questions or problems, people on the Internet are usually helpful and very forgiving if you make a mistake. The most important thing you can do is learn from your mistakes and keep going. Pretty soon, you'll be the one helping newbies learn their way around.

Making Global Connections

Do you have a friend that you've promised to visit at some point in the future? Why wait? With the Internet, you can go there now. You won't be taking a plane or car or ship to faraway destinations. Instead, you'll use your computer to meet people in foreign countries, consult maps, ask questions, and experience other cultures without even leaving home.

Your journey across the globe making connections can happen in many different ways. Here's a sneak preview of the projects in this chapter:

In *F³: Finding Foreign Friends,* you can meet and exchange e-mail with other kids around the world.

In *Exploring the Past*, you can discover remote or populated areas of the world and find out what the people's lives are like who live there.

In *Virtual Tour Book*, you can use all kinds of cool maps to help you plan the route you will take on a future journey, or look at where you've traveled in the past.

Get started on any one of the projects and see where your global connections take you!

F³: _Finding _Foreign _Friends

Making friends and learning about their interests and hobbies is something we all like to do, but where can you easily find opportunities to make friends who have different cultures, languages, and customs? The _F³: _Finding _Foreign _Friends_ project is a great way to start!

Why is the Chinese New Year _not_ celebrated on January 1? How many languages do kids in Europe learn in school? How do kids in Egypt celebrate birthdays? You may not have ever thought about these questions, but the answers might surprise you.

When you make a friend from another culture you will discover that there are a lot of things they do differently from you. You will also discover that there are a lot of things that you do exactly the same way. You will certainly never run out of questions to ask when you make a friend from another country.

The Internet features you will use in this project are e-mail, listservs, and the Web.

Finding Your Net Pal

1. Subscribe to a listserv or visit a Web site to meet people who live in other countries.

Two: Making Global Connections

A Net pal is like a pen pal, except you are using a computer and the Internet to share your thoughts and ideas instead of a paper and pen. As you can see from the list in *Places to Find Net Pals*, several different places help bring people together who have similar interests. If you want to subscribe to one of the listservs, follow the directions for subscribing in *Places to Find Net Pals*, and begin your search for fun and interesting people.

Places to Find Net Pals

Pen Pals

Send an e-mail message to this listserv at pen-pals-request@ mainstream.com and in the text of the message, type **subscribe Pen-pals** *<your name>*. (Replace *<your name>* with your first and last name.) You will receive a message confirming that you are a member of the group and further instructions on how to participate.

Kidlink Project

Send an e-mail message to this listserv at listserv@vm1.nodak.edu and in the text of the message, type **get kidlink general.** You will receive a message back confirming that you are a member of the group and further instructions on how to participate.

Places to Find Net Pals (cont.)

Cyber Kids	**Use your Web browser to go to** `http://www.mtlake.com/cyberkids/`. **Once you're there, go into the Cyberkids Connection section and follow the directions to register.**
Mighty Media's KeyPals Club	**To go to this club, point your Web browser to** `http://www.mightymedia.com,` **then click on "Keypals" and follow the directions.**

Another way to find a Net pal is to check the links that Yahooligans! posts at its category search Web page. To get there, go to `http://www`
`.yahooligans.com` and select the category "Around the World" (see Figure 2.1). You will see another list of categories appear where you'll select "People." On this new page, there is a category called "Pen Pals" which, when you click on it, will list several sites on the Web to help you find a Net pal.

TIP

When you are communicating with people over the Internet, keep a few things in mind: Check with your parents before you put personal information (like your phone number or address) in your e-mail messages. Also, if you get a message from someone you don't know or think that the message is inappropriate, don't respond to it. And finally, before you send a message, read it as if you were someone else to make sure it communicates what you want to say.

2. Post a message on at least one listserv or send a message to a specific e-mail address you found at a Web site.

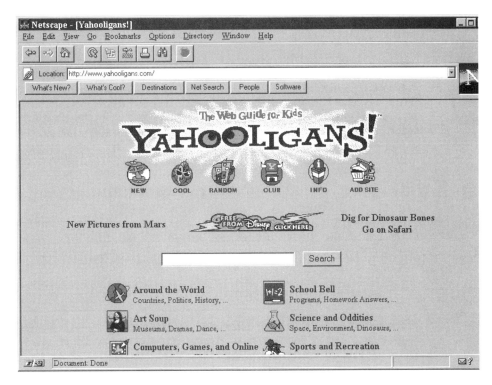

FIGURE 2.1: **Use Yahooligans! to get to other pages on the Web for finding a Net pal.** (http://www.yahooligans.com)

If you've subscribed to a listserv, write an e-mail to send to the people who subscribe to the listserv you have selected. You may have to read the directions of the listserv to see how to post a message. In your message, include questions that you want people to answer. For instance, to learn more about different cultures, you could ask a question about traditional food: "What kinds of food does your family cook for special holidays?" You could ask them what they do to have fun, what they like to watch on TV, or what they want to be when they grow up. Once you post your message, be patient—it may take a little time for everyone who is interested to read your message and send a response. And you never know where your Net pal lives. He or she might live in Florida or France or maybe even Montana or Mexico.

> As you move around the Web, you may also find that there are chat areas where you talk to a bunch of kids at one time. Remember, when you post a message to that site, *anyone* who visits that page can read your message.

3. Communicate regularly with your new Net pal.

As you start getting to know one, or maybe several Net pals, you may begin to communicate regularly. You may end up making friends for a lifetime!

> When your Net pal sends a message, answer right away. You know how much you like getting a quick response!

Once you have a Net pal, you can talk about anything you want. You can ask questions, share your writing, plan a project, play a game, and more.

Learning a New Language

If you are learning another language, try to find a Net pal who is a native speaker of the language you are studying and write your messages in that language. Don't forget to ask your Net pal to answer your questions in his or her language. You'll be amazed at how quickly you can learn a language when you are sent a personal message that you have to translate.

Two: Making Global Connections

Maybe you will want to become an exchange student and go to school in a foreign country. It certainly would be fun to visit your Net pal's country.

You don't have to have just one Net pal! Maybe you want to have several Net pals that are in different places all around the world.

HOT! HOT! HOT!

Teen Safari
http://www.discovery.com/area/nature/safari/safari1.html

Talk about making global connections! These two teen wayfarers, Jamie and Ben, took the ultimate field trip to Africa and here they share what they found.

Pen Pal Planet
http://www.epix.net/~ppplanet/page6.html

Make friends, learn about other cultures, and even improve your writing by exchanging snail mail letters with a pen pal. You can get started at this site, provided you are between 12 and 20 years old.

Yahooligans!: Pen Pal
http://www.yahooligans.com/Around_the_World/
People/Pen_Pals

Here you'll find a good list of sites that will help you to make connections with other kids around the world through the Internet.

Exploring the Past

Exploring the Past is a project that lets you design your own journey through time. By using listservs and the Web, you conduct personal interviews with people who lived through different historical periods such as the Depression, World War II, the rock 'n' roll fifties, or the hippie sixties, and the Vietnam War. Now you will have a chance to learn about everyday life in the past.

Wouldn't it be great if you owned a machine that allowed you to travel back in time? Imagine that you could see what your mother was like as a kid. Or imagine that you could travel back to a place where a recent historical or social event took place. Can you imagine what life was like 20 years ago? 30? 50? Many people can't even remember what life was like without TVs, VCRs, or computers. Can you imagine going to school in a one-room schoolhouse and doing all your math calculations on a small slate chalkboard?

Now you have your very own time machine and don't have to just *imagine* what is like...you can find out from people who were actually there!

Using the Internet, you can compare different peoples' experiences of a historical event. For example, you might want to compare what people were doing when Neil Armstrong became the first person to walk on the moon. Not only will you find out what everyday life was like in the past and what was happening in history, but you will have a chance to share the experiences of your own life today.

The Internet features you will use in this project are Telnet, listserv, and the Web.

Where you go on your journey into the past is entirely up to you. You might already be interested in a particular historical event, like the gold rush of 1850, or maybe you're just curious about what it was like to be your age at the turn of the century in the year 1900. To find people or information about people who have lived in generations other than your own, you can access a variety of Internet listservs, Web sites, and other resources. You can also check out *History Resources on the Internet*.

Gandhi's nonviolent movement helped gain independence for India in 1947 and inspired Martin Luther King Jr.'s leadership of the Civil Rights movement in the US a generation later.

Find out more about Gandhi and his philosophy of nonviolence at:

www.engagedpage

Find an event or period in recent history that interests you.

To get some historical facts about a recent historical event, you can access several different services. Figure 2.2 shows some of the things you can explore through the Library of Congress. Figure 2.3 shows the USA Government & Historical Resources home page, which was created by student Jennifer Hansen for the gradutae Library & Information Sciences Program at Wayne State University.

FIGURE 2.2: **You can search the historical collections of the Library of Congress at** `http://lcweb2.loc.gov`.

History Resources on the Internet

HNSource

Telnet to ukanaix.cc.ukans.edu **or** 129.237.33.1 **and type history.** HNSource offers access to historical events and documents.

Virtual Reference Desk

Go to gopher://gopher.libraries .wayne.edu **and click on "Politics and Government."**

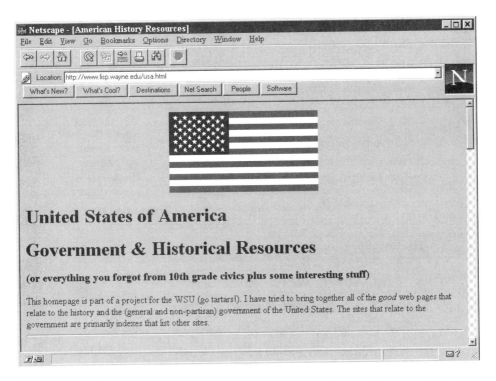

FIGURE 2.3: **This resource list will lead you to useful sites about the U.S. government and history** (http://gopher.libraries.wayne.edu/LISP/usa.html).

2. Gather information about a specific historical event or the firsthand experiences of a person from a different generation.

You can decide what you want to do first: research history or find a friend from an older generation. For sample questions that you might want to pose, see *Questions to Ask*.

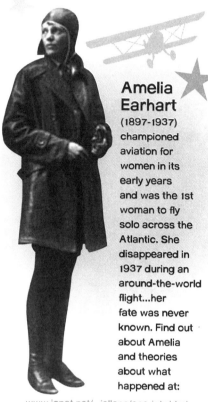

Amelia Earhart
(1897-1937) championed aviation for women in its early years and was the 1st woman to fly solo across the Atlantic. She disappeared in 1937 during an around-the-world flight...her fate was never known. Find out about Amelia and theories about what happened at:

www.ionet.net/ jellenc/eae_intr.html

Questions to Ask

When and where were you born?

What kinds of games did you play as a kid?

What was a typical day like for you at school?

What jobs did you have?

What is the most important thing that has happened in your lifetime?

3.

Find a Net pal who was living at the time of the historical event you are researching.

If you want to have an eyewitness account of events, you'll have to limit the periods you research to the 20th century. If you go back further, you'll need to check newspapers or diaries for firsthand accounts. For suggestions on historical events to investigate, check the list of *Historical Events and Eras*. You may get several responses from different people who all lived through the same event.

Post your message on one of the listservs listed in *Internet Listservs* or explore the resources on *Youth Net* (on the next page). Once you start getting responses, you'll want to think about organizing and recording the data in a creative and exciting way. Eventually you can share this information with friends in your hometown or other friends you've made through this project.

Historical Events and Eras

Famous Inventors
The Civil War
The Sinking of the Titanic
The Roaring '20s
The Depression
Early Automobiles
World War II and the Holocaust
The Rock 'n' Roll '50s
The Civil Rights Movement
The First Walk on the Moon
The Beginning of the Computer Age

Internet Listservs

Send an e-mail message to this listserv at listserv @ubvm.bitNet **and in the text of the message, type subscribe GeriNet <*your name*>. (Replace <*your name*> with your first and last name.) You will receive a message back confirming that you are a member of the group and further instructions on how to participate.**

Youth Net

Go to http://www.youth.net on the World Wide Web and click on "Memories of 1945," where a panel of WWI survivors answer students' questions.

Capoeira is martial-arts/dance form developed by escaped African slave communities in Brazil in the 1700's, and it's still hip—in fact, you can probably find a capoeira class in your community. Find out more about this tradition at www.bnbcomp.net/capoeira/capt.htm

Telling Others about Your Exploration of the Past

You will probably have your own great ideas about how to record the findings of your journey, but if you're stumped, take a look at some of these ideas:

★ Make a newspaper or report of different people's accounts of a day in history. For example, you might want to write several short articles about what people were doing when Neil Armstrong walked on the moon, or where they were the day Charles Lindbergh made the first flight across the Atlantic Ocean.

★ With the help of your friend who lived back then, create journal or diary entries that describe what life was like in the past. You could also do a mirror diary of your own that shows what life is like for you today. This might be fun for the two of you to compare.

⭐ Once you find out your new friend's birthdate, investigate everything that was happening on that day on the HNSource Web site. Make your friend a birthday card that includes this information and send it to him or her.

⭐ Imagine what everyday life will be like in the 21st century. Write a story about what people's everyday lives might be like.

Once you have created your final product, share it with others on the Internet. If you have written something, you can copy and paste your writing from your word processor to your e-mail software. Send it to the listserv and let others read about your explorations of the past.

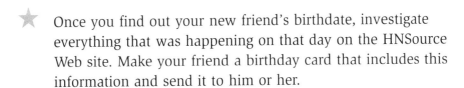

The Emily Project
`http://www.interlog.com/~amy/phpl.cgi?Emily.html`

Go to this page to read part of a woman's diary from the 1930s. Contribute to the diary or read about how this site is going about finding the original owner of the diary.

The Academy of Achievement
`http://www.achievement.org/`

This site allows you to search for extraordinary individuals who shaped the 20th century.

Electronic Classroom
`http://www.seattletimes.com/mlk/classroom.html`

Check out this site to take a quiz about Martin Luther King Jr. or read about his life and the civil rights movement.

The History Channel
`http://www.historychannel.com`

On this site you can read famous speeches from history, or you can check out "This Day in History."

Virtual Tour Book

Virtual Tour Book is a project that takes you to different Web sites that have all kinds of maps you can use to plan a future journey—or to plan an imaginary trip. Join the travel craze by making a tour book that you and your friends can use to travel the world!

Most people use maps to make sure they turn on the right roads during a trip. But for people traveling the world, like yourself, you need a whole collection of maps that can help you get from one place to the next and help you figure out where to go in a new city.

Really what you need is a tour book for your dream dream trip! In this project you will select five cities or locations in the world that you want to visit and then build a tour book that you and your friends can use when you can actually get on a plane and see the world!

The Internet feature you will use in this project is the Web.

Select five places in the world to explore.

You probably already know someone who lives in a city other than your own in the United States. Maybe your cousins live in Wichita,

Two: Making Global Connections

Kansas. Maybe a friend of yours moved to Montgomery, Alabama. You may also know people that live in another country. Maybe you have one or several Net pals. (To make some Net pals, check out the project F^3: _Finding Foreign Friends_ in this chapter.)

It helps to look at a U.S. or world atlas to get some ideas for destinations that you might find interesting. Do you like beaches and hot temperatures? Take a look at cities near the equator. Do you like playing in the snow or hiking tall mountains? Look at cities closer to the North and South Poles and around mountain ranges. Or maybe you're more interested in a specific place that's not a city. Maybe you'd like to visit a national park like Yellowstone. Or, you could plan a family trip to Disneyworld. Or find out what city Italy's Leaning Tower of Pisa is in.

Still not sure where to go? Use the suggestions in _Pick a Place Where_.

Gather information about your selected locations.

What kind of information do you need about your dream destinations? Check out _Questions to Answer in Your Tour Book_ to help narrow down the information you need.

Pick a Place Where:

- you or a relative was born

- there is a unique geological land formation, such as the African Sahara Desert, the Grand Canyon in Arizona, the Mountains of Nepal, the volcanoes in the South Pacific islands

- there's a national park, such as Montana's Glacier National Park or California's Yosemite National Park

- your favorite story is set

- your favorite famous person was born

- you would like to go on your next vacation, such as Disneyland

- a relative or friend lives

- a historical landmark is, such as the Leaning Tower of Pisa

- a historical event happened, such as where gold was discovered in California

59

Questions to Answer in Your Tour Book

How do you get to each city or location? Is it by car, bus, plane, train, boat, or even bicycle? Does it change between different places?

What unique sites are in the city? Is there an amazing tower, museum, or park?

What kind of clothes will you need to bring for each city? Is it sweltering heat or cool breezes? Do you need a swim suit or a down parka?

What language do they speak in that place?

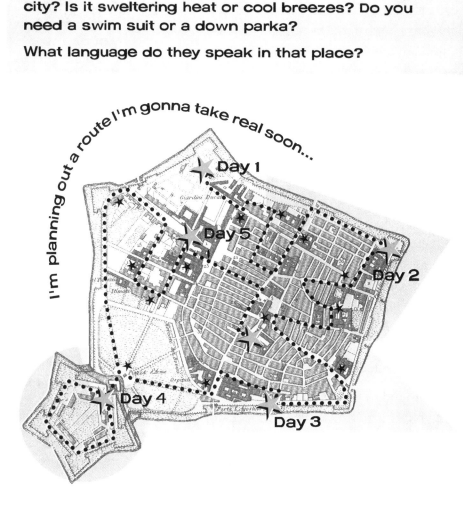

I'm planning out a route I'm gonna take real soon...

Day 1
Day 5
Day 2
Day 4
Day 3

Now take a look at *Mapping It Out on the Web*. This is where you will find several amazing places to look at maps of cities all around the world. Included in this list of helpful Web sites is the World Factbook, which includes all kinds of specific information about every country in the world. This is where you can find information like average temperatures, spoken languages, and available transportation. You can also go to Atlapedia Online, which contains profiles of every country in the world from A to Z (http://www.atlapedia.com).

Mapping It Out On the Web

World Factbook
http://cliffie.nosc.mil/~NATLAS/wfb/index.html

This source is maintained by the CIA and includes detailed information about locations around the world.

Mapquest
http://www.mapquest.com

You can use this site to see your own street as well as streets in cities in every country.

The Great Globe Gallery
http://hum.amu.edu.pl/~zbzw/glob/glob0.htm

This site has a lot of graphics of globes and maps including a satellite image of the earth.

Historical Maps of the United States
http://www.lib.utexas.edu/Libs/PCL/Map_collection/histus.html

This University of Texas collection of maps makes a great resource for learning about the history of the United States.

The Heritage Map Museum
http://www.carto.com/index.htm

This virtual museum holds tons of maps that show you the world the way it looked 50 or 100 years ago.

3. Search the Web for sites specifically designed for your destination.

To see if there are any sites on the Web that deal with your dream cities specifically, you can conduct a search. If you need some help doing this, check out the section in Chapter 1 that tells you some great sites to go to for your search.

> **TIP**
>
> Most of the search tools listed in Chapter 1 have a travel category that contains links to all kinds of travel-related Web sites.

When you do this, you may find maps, pictures of local art, local events, and all kinds of other things that people have published on the Web (see Figure 2.4).

4. Make a tour book for you and your friends.

Congratulations! You now have a large amount of information with which to create your tour book. As you continue to explore the Internet, you may come across other resources that have additional information about your dream cities. You can always update your tour book when you learn something new.

Publishing Your Tour Book

Once you have finished mapping out your adventure, you can share your tour book with people around the country or even around the world. Send your map by postal service to someone you may know who lives in the state or city you studied to see what they think of it.

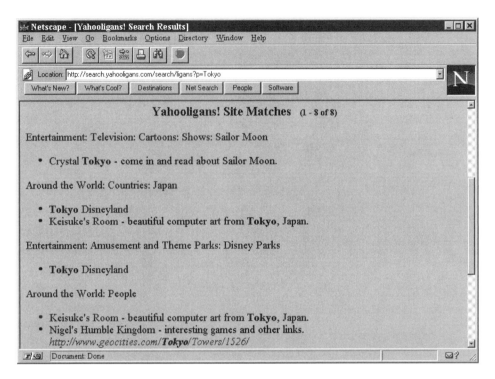

FIGURE 2.4: **A bunch of different information is found on Tokyo, Japan, by conducting a search using Yahooligans!**

As you get into building your own Web pages (see Chapter 9 for more information), you can publish your tour book on the Web so that other people can plan their own trips based on the information you collect.

When you finally do make your dream trip and visit your selected cities, the people you meet will be surprised when they find out how much you know about places far away from your own!

HOT! HOT! HOT!

Travelocity
http://www.travelocity.com

Be sure to click on Destinations and Interests to find a spot in the world to visit.

Expedia
http://www.expedia.msn.com/wg/

To find the best restaurant or the museum's hours, check out Expedia.

Lonely Planet Travel Guides
http://www.lonelyplanet.com

Read the comprehensive travel guides, get in touch with other travelers, even add your two cents to the guide books or send a multimedia postcard.

The National Park Service
http://www.nps.gov

Whether you want to relive a prior trip to a national park or plan a future one, this site has all you need to know. Learn about the wildlife, the environment and what trails or camping sites are available for you to experience the great outdoors!

Disneyland/DisneyWorld
http://www.disney.com

Everything you wanted to know about these world famous places for fun and magic is found at this site. Mickey always rolls out the red carpet for his guests!

HOT! HOT! HOT!

**Univ. of Iowa-Center for Global & Regional
Environmental Research**
http://www.cgrer.uiowa.edu/servers/
servers-reference.html

**One aspect of environmental research is the need
to create and update maps for many different outdoor locations. Thanks to the University of Iowa
you get to see them on the Web!**

**SeaWorld/Busch Gardens Animal
Information Database**
http://www.seaworld.org

**Check out the shark cam to see 32 sharks and
learn more about them.**

Loteria
37
EL MUNDO
BINGO!
I think...
pick a card, any card...
GREAT
GAMES
MUSELANDIA
Hail, Steveth!
Hail, Gweneth!
Wrong Again, Bear Breath! Lose a Turn.
go ahead, tease my brain...
Oh Bother!
Try twisting the top layer two times...

Great Games and Perfect Puzzles on the Net

L ike playing games? The Internet has an amazing amount of games for you to have fun and test your skills and knowledge. Whether you play against a computer or find yourself in a virtual room of competitors, the projects in this chapter will definitely put you to the test. Take a walk on the wild side of the Internet, where you can match wits and nerves with both humans and computers alike:

★ *Classic Games on the Web* shows you where to go to play games that you may already know—like backgammon, checkers, and chess.

★ *Test Your Brain* with trivia and puzzles that will be so much fun, you won't even notice that you've learned something!

Classic Games on the Web

Now there are global game boards for classic games like chess, checkers, and backgammon. Formidable opponents are somewhere in the world, and you can use the Net to play against them. This is a project where you can find your favorite games on the Internet, whether you are a beginner or an expert.

Do you like to play chess, checkers, Battleship, or Scrabble? You'll soon find that there are tons of cool game sites on the Internet! This is your chance to become an expert at your favorite game—and to discover new games to have fun playing. With the Internet, you can really test your skill as an opponent.

The Internet feature you will need for this project is the Web.

Playing the Games

1. Access the Web sites of your choice and learn the game rules and terminology.

Once you reach a site listed in *Internet Game Sites* and learn how matches are played, you'll probably find a whole new set of rules and terms for playing your game online. For example, if you decide to compete on the Internet in chess, you'll have to learn the computer code names for king, queen, rooks, and knights as well as the codes for making moves. Playing a game online adds new dimensions to old strategies!

TIP

You may need to download some games before you can play them. This may take a few minutes, but be patient. You may also be instructed to download another piece of software, like Java, before you can really play the game. Go ahead and download the game or software, but be sure to run them through a virus-checking program before you open them. (See Chapter 1 for more about downloading.)

Internet Game Sites

PlaySite
http://www.playsite.com

Challenge someone to a game of chess, checkers, reversi, or backgammon.

Internet Game Sites (cont.)

Java on the brain
http://www.tdb.uu.se/~karl/brain.html

See one person's collection of games developed with the Java programming language.

Web Mine Sweeper
http://info.gte.com/gtel/fun/mines/mines.html

To make your way through this mine field, you will have to use your head.

Kinglink Games
http://www.kinglink.com/gameforum.html

There are many different types of games here, but be sure not to miss Dino Numbers and Dino Spell, two games that will improve your math and spelling skills while you have fun.

Games Domain
http://www.gamesdomain.com/tigger/index.html

Here at the Games Domain, you can read game reviews, download games, and enter contests. You can even get cool graphics.

Zarf's Ex-List of Interactive Games on the Web
http://www.leftfoot.com/realgames.html#games

Games, games, games! This site has everything from Tic-Tac-Toe to trivia.

2. Play your game.

Each site is going to have a different set of instructions; for example, see those shown in Figure 3.1. The nice thing about playing a game on the Internet is that you can take your time and strategize about the best move to make. This way the fun of the game is stretched out over days or maybe even weeks.

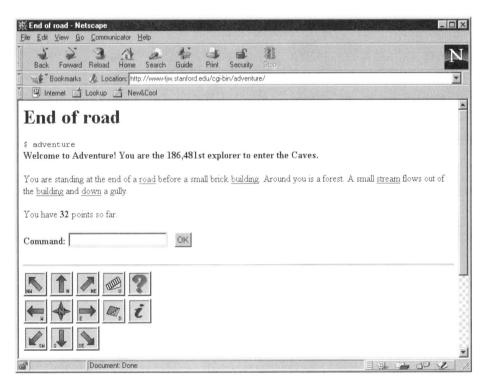

FIGURE 3.1: **Explore unknown worlds and test your courage in the interactive fantasy game Adventure** (http://www-tjw.stanford.edu/adventure).

HOT! HOT! HOT!

Funstuff
http://info.gte.com/gtel/fun

Provided by GTE laboratories, this site includes the Web games of Battleship, Mine Sweeper, Rubik's Magic Cube, and A Virtual Maze.

Board Games
http://alabanza.com/kabacoff/InterLinks/fun/b_games.html

From this site you can play backgammon, chess, Go (a Korean game), Scrabble, and XiangQi (Chinese chess).

Tic-Tac-Toe
http://netpressence.com/npcgi/ttt

It's an old standard game but one that be very addicting!

Develcor
http://www.develcor.com

This site includes games, such as Battleship, Checkers, and so on, that you can download and then play against other people online, or against your own computer.

Yahooligans! and Yahoo! Game Indexes
http://www.yahooligans.com **and** http://www.yahoo.com

Click on the games category to get a list of hundreds of fun games to play on the Internet.

Test Your Brain

Did you hear about the chess match between world champion Gary Kasparov and Deep Blue, IBM's chess-playing computer? What's amazing about computers is that you can play games against them. And, just like when you play against your friends, it is always a challenge.

Playing a game by yourself doesn't have to be boring; when you match wits with a computer, you can learn a lot and have fun.

The Internet today has more learning games than you can play in a lifetime. These learning games generally fall into two categories: trivia games and visual puzzles. You can also decide what sort of setting you want to play in—say, a medieval castle or a spaceship—and what sort of information you want to learn—for instance, spelling, history, and even sports trivia.

The Internet feature you will use in this project is the Web.

Let Your Brain Play

Thinking is fun, especially when you are challenged in a game!

1. Decide what sort of "thinking game" you want to play.

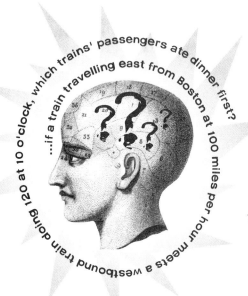

...if a train travelling east from Boston at 100 miles per hour meets a westbound train doing 120 at 10 o'clock, which trains' passengers ate dinner first?

Thinking games can be puzzles, sometimes called *brain teasers*, or trivia games. Which do you prefer? Do you want to test your visual skills as you attempt to re-assemble a picture of the Statue of Liberty like the one in Figure 3.2? How about solving a visual puzzle that will require a keen eye and concentration? This is the time to decide, and a good place to start is one of the sites listed in this project—you will have lots to choose from.

2. Just do it.

Play hard, but remember: It's just a game. In Figure 3.3 you can see how challenging the trivia games can be.

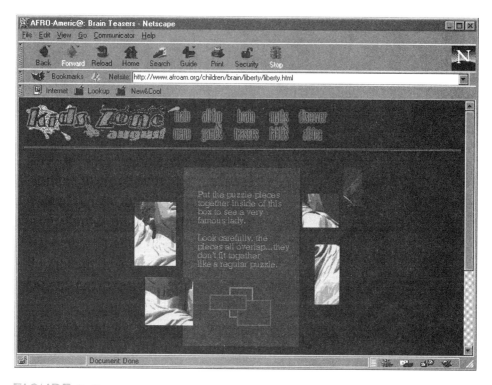

FIGURE 3.2: **Think you can put the Lady Liberty back together? Try it at the African American Kids Zone** (`http://www.afroam.org/children/brain/liberty/liberty.html`).

3. Keep track of your scores.

Every time you play a certain game, make a note of your score (or your time). Over time, you will notice that you are improving! You can also challenge your friends to play and then compare scores.

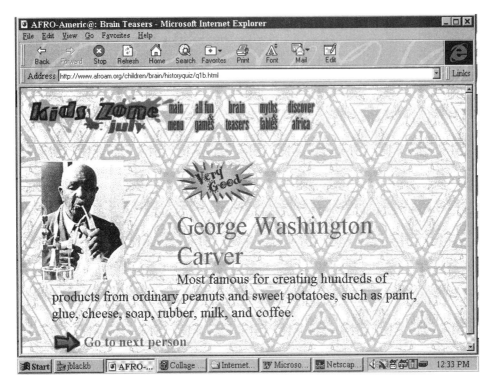

FIGURE 3.3: **Trivia games are a great way to test your knowledge. This is the Black History Quiz** (http://www.afroam.org/children/brain/historyquiz/q1.html)**.**

4. Use the Web to learn more.

You can improve your scores on those trivia games by seeking out related information on the Web. For example, if your scores in dinosaur trivia are lagging, brush up on your dino-facts at one of many sites out there on the Internet.

HOT! HOT! HOT!

Happy Puppy Kidz Page
http://www.happypuppy.com/kidz/

You'll be a happy puppy when you see this vast archive of free games—everything from brain teasers to 3-D action games!

Cyberkids
http://www.cyberkids.com

This site not only has a reading room and an art gallery, but it also has lots of great games, such as the Egyptian Word Search. You work with many of these games by printing them out and playing them without your computer.

Bonus.com
http://www.bonus.com

At this site you can choose from many games. Plus, you can win prizes.

African American Kids Zone
http://ww.afroam.org/children/children.html

This site is especially rich in brain teasers and informative trivia games. You can go here to learn about African-American culture.

The GeoNet Game
http://www.hmco.com/hmco/school/geo/indexhi.html

Play this game where you think and learn geographically.

Changing the World...with a Few Friends

Everyone has opinions about how to make the world a better place to live. Sometimes you have such strong opinions that you want to share them with others or take some kind of action to let people know how you feel. The more people expressing ideas, the greater the chance there is for change. In this chapter, you will find projects that will give you a variety of opportunities to express your opinions to others, as well as communicate with people who can make the changes you want:

★ *Voicing Your Opinions* is a great opportunity for you to learn about issues affecting kids in your community, learn how kids around the world are dealing with that issue, and communicate your opinions to people who can influence or make changes.

★ *Finding a Cure* is packed with ideas for how you can help kids your age who are battling diseases.

★ *Artistic Reflections* is the project for you if you use art or music to express your opinions.

By putting your ideas together with other kids' ideas, you can change the world!

Voicing Your Opinions

NOTE

Is there something going on in your city or country that you don't like? Do you think something should be done differently? *Voicing Your Opinions* will give you ideas about speaking your opinions, making suggestions, and getting to know other people who may agree or disagree with you. You can join together with other people to really solve a problem.

What would you do if someone in your community suggested that it would be cheaper for the city if they stopped collecting items for recycling? Instead of putting your glass bottles, newspapers, and aluminum cans in recycling bins so they could be picked up and used to create new products, they would be taken to landfills because recycling centers cost too much money to run. What is the right decision for the community? Is there anything you can do about it?

The Internet gives you a way to do something: Say what you think to people who can make changes. If you don't like what's happening at your school, you can try to convince the school leaders to change their minds. If you are concerned about an issue in your town, you can share your ideas with the city or town council. Politicians in your state and in the country (even including the President of the United States!) are interested to know your ideas on issues that affect you and other kids.

The Internet features you will use for this project are e-mail, Gopher, and the Web.

Steps for Change

If you want to make your point and be effective, you need to be informed. Here's a way to use all kinds of resources on the Internet to inform yourself about issues affecting your life.

1. Identify a local issue affecting you and other kids in your community.

Maybe recycling isn't an issue in your community, but there's bound to be something that you and your friends would like to change. Does your town need better bike paths? Does your school need more computers? What changes would your friends like to see in your community or school?

Finding news online is easy. Every month, there are more and more news-gathering organizations putting up Web sites. Sites like Yahooligans! and Excite provide special categories devoted to online newspapers. Be sure to check out *Networked News* in Chapter 7.

To help gather information and look at various issues going on around you, you can also read articles in the local paper to find out what other people in the town think are issues of importance. In particular, read the editorial pages where the editors of the paper write how they feel about certain issues, national and local. These pages also include letters from members of the community that may agree or disagree with a previous day's editorials. You can even check with your local newspaper to see if it's online.

2. Find out if kids in other communities are experiencing similar issues.

A great thing about the Internet is that you can find other kids who are struggling with the same issue that you and your friends are facing. To find them requires a little patience and creativity, but you're sure to have fun along the way.

To find other communities and people, you can conduct a search of the Web around your issue. The first thing you will need to do is decide which tool to use for your keyword search. At the Too Cool for Grownups site (`http://www.tcfg.com/racers.html`), there is an area called "Racers, Start Your Engines" where you can read the descriptions of search tools and pick one that's right for the job (see Figure 4.1). The descriptions will tell you the advantages and disadvantages of each.

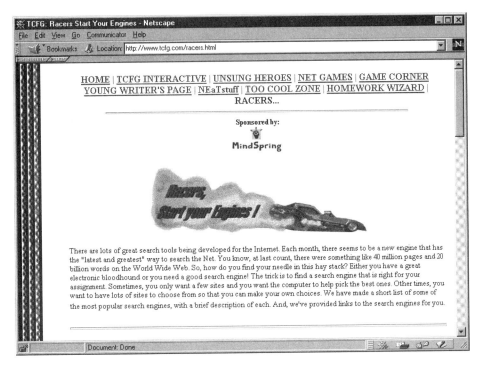

FIGURE 4.1: **Too Cool for Grownups offers a great collection of search tools to help you find information on the Web** (http://www.tcfg.com/racers.html).

Once you have selected a tool, think about a specific keyword that will help you find information about your issue. For example, if you are interested in finding kids to talk to about recycling, you might conduct a search using "recycling." Or, if you are concerned about the lack of bicycle paths, you can conduct a search for "bicycle paths" or "bike paths." Thinking of different variations of words can help

generate better search results. For example, if you're looking for ways to start a recycling program in your school, you could try these keywords in different combinations:

recycle

school

recycling

recycling program

Most search engines provide tips for creating the keyword or keywords that will bring you the most appropriate matching links. Look for a Help button to find out more about a particular search engine's techniques.

3. Discover strategies that kids in other communities are using to resolve their issues.

There are several great places to go on the Web where kids are talking about the issues affecting them and their friends. When you visit any site in *Youth Issue Sites*, you can read about what other kids are thinking and maybe even have a conversation with them across the computer. One of these sites is from UNICEF, which is a primary international organization concerned with the challenges of youth around the world.

Youth Issue Sites

Voices of Youth
http://www.unicef.org/voy

This site is part of UNICEF, the United Nations Children's Fund, which is a worldwide organization dedicated to kids of all ages.

Youth In Action
http://www.mightymedia.com/act

This site is a great network of youth trying to make the world a better place.

4. Take action that you think will help your community address the issue.

While you are searching and exploring the Web, keep a list of the strategies you find other kids using to influence change where they live. They might be circulating petitions, writing letters to the newspaper, or making speeches at the city council or school board meetings. Will one of these strategies work for your group? When a group of local youth present ideas that they believe will improve the city, people tend to listen.

Maybe your local leaders can't solve your issue. Maybe you have to go to the top for change to happen—you know, Congress or the President! If so, there are lots of resources you can use to get information and voice your opinions. For example, you can use the Legislate Gopher Service (see Figure 4.2 and the *Legislate Gopher Service* sidebar) to see the current topics of discussion in the U.S. Congress.

When you have an idea for a new or improved law, you can send an electronic message to a local representative or the President of the United States that describes your concerns and suggestions.

Send your e-mail message to one of the addresses listed in *Internet Addresses for Congress and the White House.* There is also a listing of congressional addresses you can have sent to you by e-mail. Figure 4.3 shows the home map for the White House for Kids Web site, which includes a way for you to voice your opinion.

Legislate Gopher Service

Use your Web browser to go to gopher:// gopher.legislate.com. **Choose "Legislation (Bills & Resolutions)" and then the topmost folder for the latest legislative information on the current session of Congress. You will get directions for searching either by a Congressperson's name, the name of a bill, or a keyword like "crime."**

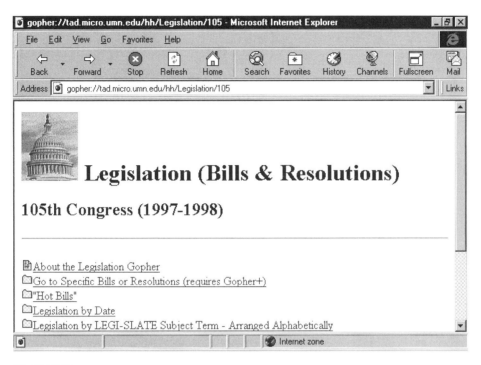

FIGURE 4.2: **Here is the list of topics for the 105th Congress from the Legislate Gopher Service.**

Internet Addresses for Congress and the White House

If you want to send your local senator or representative an e-mail, use this service to find their e-mail addresses: http://webcom.com/~leavitt/cong.html

If you want to send the President or Vice President an e-mail, check the White House for Kids Web site: http://www.whitehouse.gov/WH/kids/html/home.html

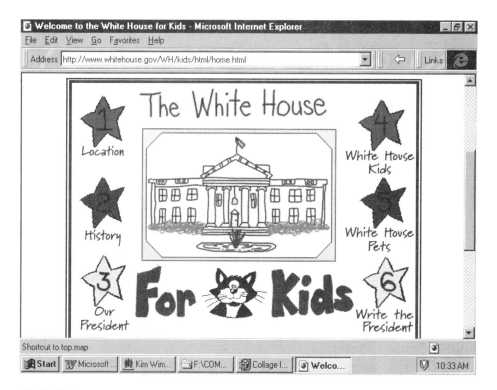

FIGURE 4.3: Send your note right to the President and Vice President from the White House for Kids Web site (http://www.whitehouse.gov/WH/kids/html/home.html).

HOT! HOT! HOT!

White House for Kids
http://www.whitehouse.gov/WH/kids/html/home.html

Learn more about the workings of the federal branch of government and in a way that makes sense. E-mail addresses for the President, First Lady, and Vice President are included, too!

HOT! HOT! HOT!

Government Information Locator
`http://www.law.vill.edu/fed-agency/fedwebloc.html`

Here you can search for mailing addresses and information about the people running the federal government like senators, representatives, and agency leaders.

CapWeb, A Guide to the U.S. Congress
`http://policy.net/capweb/congress.html`

Explore the U.S. government via links to the Senate, House of Representatives, and the Library of Congress, with additional resources on the executive and judicial branches of the federal government.

Environmental Protection Agency's Web Site for Students and Teachers
`http://www.epa.gov/epahome/students.htm`

Find facts about the environment as well as links to other environmental sites on the Web. Facts are organized around current issues such as clean air, hazardous waste, and ozone depletion.

Finding a Cure

Remember the last time you were sick? It probably wasn't a whole lot of fun and you did everything you could to get better like sleeping, taking medicine, eating healthy food, and drinking a lot of orange juice! Bet you were happy when you felt better and could get out of the house again.

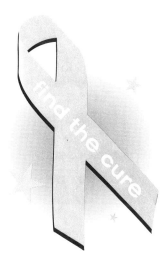

Information is power. *Finding a Cure* gives you ideas for getting information about diseases and disabilities that affect young people. You can educate yourself by exploring the wealth of information provided on the Internet by several organizations committed to wiping out different diseases. You can talk with people living with these challenges, medical professionals, and organizations working on finding cures and helping people.

Unfortunately, there are a lot of kids (and adults) in the world that have an illness that won't get better. They have been infected with an incurable disease or deal with a physical disability like the examples shown in *Diseases and Disabilities*. Maybe you know someone. Maybe you can find a way to help or learn more about the disease on the Internet.

For many diseases, cures have been found. To develop these cures, scientists, doctors, and many other people shared their knowledge and creativity. People learned about the disease so they could help prevent its spread. The people who are working toward a cure for diseases are confident that one can be found if people work together, share ideas, and help others.

You can help by educating yourself and others in your community about the disease. In this project, you will talk through the Internet with kids your age who are battling different diseases or disabilities as well as with doctors and scientists that are working on a cure.

Diseases and Disabilities

Juvenile Arthritis

Leukemia

Hearing or Sight Impairment

Cancer

AIDS

Multiple Sclerosis

Down's Syndrome

The Internet features you will use are Gopher and the Web.

Educating Yourself and Others

Before you can help others understand a disease or disability, you need to know the facts yourself. Sometimes there are a lot of rumors and myths about how you get a disease or how smart a disabled person really is. You can separate rumors from truth by following these steps.

1. Get updated information and statistics.

Things change quickly for the scientific and medical community working on a cure for diseases. New treatments that scientists think might slow a virus or even stop it are approved for experimentation. Scientists learn more all the time about how diseases are contracted. Possible cures are being tested in laboratories all over the world.

To keep up with these changes, visit the places listed in *Information about Diseases and Disabilities*. Here is a list of organizations that maintain resources for the public:

★ National Institute for Allergies and Infectious Diseases (NIAID)

★ Centers for Disease Control (CDC)

★ Federal Drug Administration (FDA)

Department of Education, Office of Special Education

 Department of Labor, Workforce Disabilities

Information about Diseases and Disabilities

The National Institute of Allergy and Infectious Diseases (NIAID)
gopher://odie.niaid.nih.gov

Choose "AIDS Related Information" from the menu. The site includes the National AIDS Clearinghouse from the Centers for Disease Control, plus lots of information on other diseases.

Food and Drug Administration
http://www.fda.gov

Check out this site for information about medicines and drugs.

The Body Home Page
http://www.thebody.com

Go here for information and resources for patients and their families and friends.

Healthfinder
http://www.healthfinder.gov

Healthfinder connects you to great resources and information.

Family Village
http://familyvillage.wisc.edu

Family Village offers a large collection of disability-related resources.

These organizations are all agencies of the U.S. government that are committed to providing up-to-date and reliable information on different diseases. In addition to federal agencies that collect and share information, there are also state and local groups that focus on the needs of particular geographic regions. Maybe there is an organization in your state or town that can help you learn more about a specific disease or disability. Figure 4.4 shows the main page for healthfinder, a great resource for information.

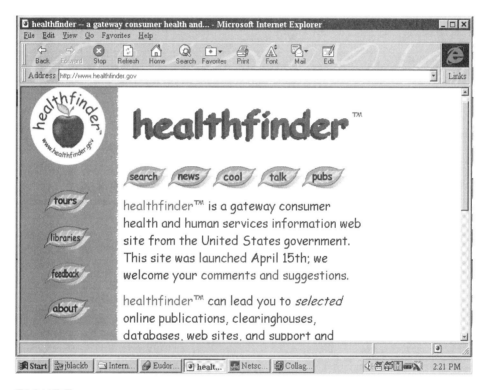

FIGURE 4.4: **Healthfinder is a great place to go for information and links to organizations in the disability and health care fields** (http://www.healthfinder.gov).

2. Talk to kids that are affected by disease or disability.

Many kids that are battling an illness or disability feel isolated and alone because none of their friends are going through the same experience. In fact, some of them even have to go to a school at a hospital, away from their friends and sometimes even family.

There are several listservs, Usenet groups, and Web sites where you can meet and talk to these kids. You can develop new friendships while also learning a lot about what it is like to live with a disease or disability. Check out the places listed in *Talking to Other Kids*.

Talking to Other Kids

Kids' Home at the National Cancer Institute
`http://icic.nci.nig.gov/occdocs/KidsHome.html`

Connect with kids with all different types of cancer.

Convomania
`http://www.mania.apple.com`

Convomania provides an "OK" place to not be "OK." Apple Computer sponsors this site as a place for seriously ill and disabled kids to chat, share artwork, and have straight talk about tough issues.

Deaf CyberKids
`http://dww.deafworldweb.org/kids`

This is a place to share ideas and feelings about being deaf. This site includes information for subscribing to a DEAFKIDS listserv.

Ability OnLine Support Network
`http://www.ablelink.org`

Connect to young people with disabilities or chronic illnesses.

3. Write a report or create a pamphlet for kids your age that describes the information you found.

As you have probably discovered in your exploration of places on the Web and your conversations with people, the human body is an incredibly complex system with a lot of different variables. Sometimes bodies react differently to the same disease.

You can help other kids understand a particular disability or disease better by writing a report and posting it on the Internet, or creating a short brochure for them. Although it may seem difficult to put all the facts you've learned into a pamphlet, you can focus on including only the most important facts and talk about them in your own words. With the brochure you can teach people something they probably don't already know.

4. Use your report for a class project, or print and distribute your pamphlet.

Once you've written your report or printed your brochure, you might want to share it with your teacher or classmates. Use it for a class project or assignment. Sharing the information you found will help spread awareness about the topic. Update your report or pamphlet periodically to keep up with new breakthroughs in research.

HOT! HOT! HOT!

Food and Drug Administration's Teen Scene
http://www.fda.gov/opacom/7teens.html

Get information about a variety of health issues that affect teens, particularly drug-related health problems.

How You Can Help
http://www.educational.net/charity.htm

Want to volunteer your time and energy to helping kids with diseases and disabilities? Use this list of charities to find the group you would more like to work with and then link to that group's own Web site.

Children's Care Hospital & School
http://www.cchs.org/kids.html

Many children attend school at the hospital if they are there for a long time. Visit this site to learn more about the challenges these kids face.

Artistic Reflections

NOTE

People see and feel different things when they look at a piece of art, and often it is very different from what the artist felt while creating it. However, art definitely evokes feelings in everyone. *Artistic Reflections* will help you find places on the Internet where you can see and learn about different types and styles of art to give you ideas about how to create your own style of artistic expression.

What do sculptors, painters, and musicians have in common? Art! They use all kinds of media—such as words, paint, music, or clay—to create artistic pieces that express their feelings and opinions. No matter how unique your ideas, no matter what medium you use to create art, there are other people on the Internet who share your interest in expressing themselves through art.

How can you use art to express your feelings? How can you make a statement and voice an opinion about life? To answer questions like these, it will be helpful to learn about other artists and their work through the Internet. You can get ideas about creating art and gain an appreciation for the contributions of other artists.

The Internet features you will use in this project are the Web and listservs.

Finding Art on the Internet

1. Choose one form of art you want to explore on the Internet.

There are so many different types of art that you will want to begin with your favorite. For instance, you might want to explore sculptures, paintings, or music by searching for files, pictures, or sounds on the Internet. You can also look at the musical side of art by searching for types of music, such as jazz, rock, blues, or classical.

2. Get examples of art from various sources on the Internet.

You will be amazed at the many sources on the Internet where you can find pictures of works of art, text files of lyrics, critical reviews of artists, and other information related to art. The information is available in different formats— graphic, text, and sound.

You may need special software on your home computer to view images or listen to sounds. If this is the case, most sites will post a note about it and either include the software at the site's Internet address or tell you where to go to get the software. If you have any problems, ask your network administrator or your parents.

In *Art Resources on the Internet* there are several different resources that contain thousands of images of works of art. One may be more useful than another depending on what type of art you are looking for. For example, the art found in the Vatican Library may be religious in nature because the Catholic Church maintains this library. The Louvre, a huge museum in Paris, includes works by many European artists. See Figure 4.5 for a picture of original artwork from the SITO Project.

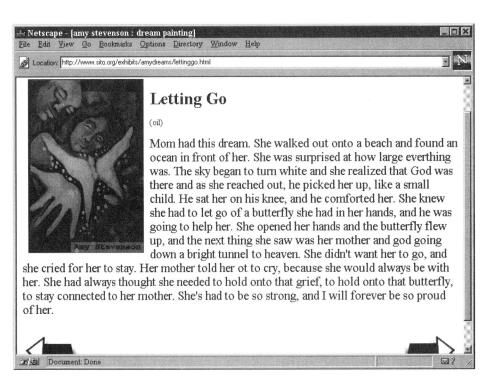

FIGURE 4.5: You can find beautiful artwork at the SITO Project (http://www.sito.org).

Art Resources on the Internet

Smithsonian Online
http://www.si.edu

National Museum of American Art
http://www.nmaa.si.edu

The Louvre Exhibits
http://mistral.enst.fr/~pioch/louvre/

The SITO Project
http://www.sito.org

Library of Congress Vatican Exhibit
http://sunsite.unc.edu/expo/vatican.exhibit/
exhibit/Main_Hall.html

ArtsEdNet
http://www.artsednet.getty.edu

TIP

Graphic files can be huge, which means they might take a long time to download. If you are going to try it, you should probably have at least a 28.8bps modem (that's the speed at which the modem sends and receives data).

Music is a popular form of art because you can experience it in so many different ways. You can sing, play an instrument, write lyrics, choreograph a dance, or just listen to the music. Use the listings in *Music Resources on the Internet* to research a type of music you don't know about or one that you don't listen to very often. (See Figure 4.6 for an introduction to the world of jazz music.) You may develop a whole new perspective on classical, rap, country, or even operatic music!

Music Resources on the Internet

Allmusic
subscribe to listserv@american.edu

WNUR-FM JazzWeb Information Server
http://www.nwu.edu/wnur/jazz

MTV Online
http://mtv.com

Music Previews Network
http://www.previews.net

Rock and Roll Hall of Fame
http://www.rockhall.com

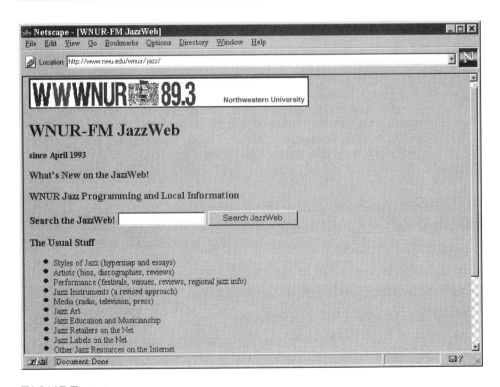

FIGURE 4.6: **Learn all about jazz music at JazzWeb**
(http://www.nwu.edu/wnur/jazz).

3. Choose one artist or one style of art and find as much information as you can.

You may already know what kind of art or which artist you want to find on the Net. If so, use a search tool to locate sites dedicated to that type of art or artist. Type in the full name of the musician or band; for instance **Janet Jackson**.

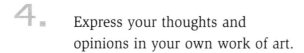

TIP

If you use the category search provided by a search engine and go into entertainment or music categories, you will find links to information about bands, music labels, and other musical topics.

If you have a favorite artist—such as a painter, sculptor, or musician—or one style of art—such as pencil drawings, watercolors, or country music—search the Internet resources for information to expand your knowledge of the person or style.

4. Express your thoughts and opinions in your own work of art.

Learning about another person's experiences can often give you ideas to draw from to create your own style. For example, growing up near an ocean may influence an artist's style or even the subjects of his or her art. By creating art, you can express your opinion about something or even introduce someone else to that particular form of art.

Artistic Collaboration

Art does not have to be created by only one person. In fact, it takes hundreds of people to create a musical play or to design and build a beautiful church or temple. These are a few examples of collaborative works of art that reflect an entire community of people.

Do you have a community of artists? Are you in a drama club? Do you and your friends like to paint? Use the talents and strengths of all your friends to create an artistic expression of the group's feelings.

The most important thing you can do with your own artistic creations is to share them with others. Let people see and experience your art. Perhaps your library or museum displays art from local artists.

HOT! HOT! HOT!

CyberKids
http://www.mtlake.com/cyberkids

This is a cool place for kids to hang out and have fun. A free online magazine contains stories and artwork created by kids.

Global Show-n-Tell
http://www.manymedia.com/show-n-tell

This virtual exhibition lets kids show off their favorite projects, possessions, accomplishments, and collections to other kids around the world.

HOT! HOT! HOT!

ArtsWire
http://www.artswire.org/

Search the "WebBase" at ArtsWire to find all kinds of information about an area of fine arts such as dance, theater, sculpture, and painting.

Movie Makers Guild
http://www.el-dorado.co.us/~dmnews/mmguild.html

Learn how to create storyboards which are the road map for the hit movie you now have in your head. Real movie makers share ideas and ask for your help at this site.

The NoodleHead Network
http://www.noodlehead.com/about/about.html

Sponsored by an award-winning video company that creates videos from a kid's eye view, this site takes you through the different phases of making a video using a basic camcorder.

Getting the Answer...Now!

When you've got a burning question and you need to find the answer, where do you go, who do you call? You've asked your friends. You've asked your teacher. You've checked the library. But no one seems to know the answer to your question. This is a job for the Internet. The projects in this chapter direct you to helpful resources that answer specific questions and help find places that match your own personal interests:

★ *I Want to Know...* provides you with step-by-step instructions for conducting research on the Internet.

★ *Writer's Corner* gives you ideas for jump-starting your brain with new and interesting ideas for writing.

★ *It's My Thing* gives you new places to play. You can find information on anything from sports to cooking to art.

I Want to Know...

Have a question that you want or need to answer? Chances are very good that you can answer it with a few keystrokes on your computer while connected to the Internet. In fact, you may become overwhelmed with the amount of information you receive. When this happens, it is important to make decisions about which sites provide information that relates most directly to your question and which sites provide the most reliable information. Although the Internet is a great source of information, it does not contain all the information in the world (yet). Sometimes a public library might yield information not available through the Internet.

The Internet feature you will use for this project is the Web.

Asking Your Question

Often you start a search on the Web with a very specific question, such as "What are the three most endangered species in North America?" only to find yourself over- whelmed with a list of thousands of sites with information that relates to your ques- tion in some way. You may see sites that have a definition of what is required to be identified as an endangered species, the geography of North America, and perhaps debates between conservationists and local hunters and fishermen. But what's the answer to your question? Follow the steps below to see the different ways to really find the answer, without spend- ing two weeks straight at your computer.

1. Think of a question and then turn it into something that the computer can understand.

In the future, scientists predict that you will be able to ask the computer your exact question and the computer will know exactly what you are looking for. Unfortunately, the computer that you have at home today isn't that smart. It doesn't speak the same language you do, so when you ask it to search for information, you have to pose the question in its language, not yours. Does this mean you have to become a computer program- mer? Definitely not!

Let's take the question "What are the three most endangered species in North America?" There are several approaches you can take to put this into the computer's language.

Using Keywords

KEYWORD

A *keyword* is one word that describes your area of interest. For example, using the question above, a good keyword might be **endangered**. As you can see in Figure 5.1, the search engine returned a list of more than 100,000 sites that contain the word **endangered**. That's a lot of sites to look at, so you can narrow down your search by adding other keywords to build a phrase.

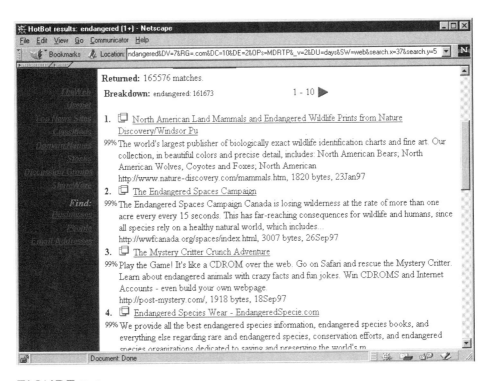

FIGURE 5.1: **The results of a search using the search tool called Hotbot and entering only the word endangered for the search.**

Using Phrases

If one word brings you too many sites to choose from, try searching for an entire phrase such as **endangered species**. As you can see in Figure 5.2, this search, using the same tool, produced a list of about 50,000 less sites.

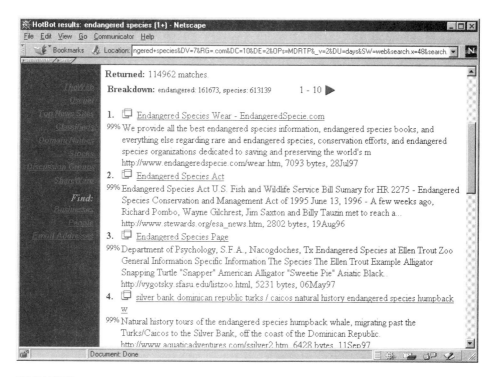

FIGURE 5.2: **The results of a search using the search tool called Hotbot and entering only the phrase endangered species for the search.**

That's still a lot to go through! At this point, you can continue to add words that may help narrow the search. For example, by adding the phrase **North America** to the search for **endangered species** a more appropriate set of sites comes back in the list as shown in Figure 5.3.

Make sure you add the word "and" or the plus sign (+) so that the search engine knows you are combining these two phrases.

TIP

When searching for a phrase where you want the words in a certain order, enclose the phrase in quotes. For instance, a search for **New York Yankees** returns all pages with any or all of those words, in any order, somewhere on the page (with pages containing all the words ranked higher of course). But a search for **"New York Yankees"** finds just the pages with that exact phrase on the page.

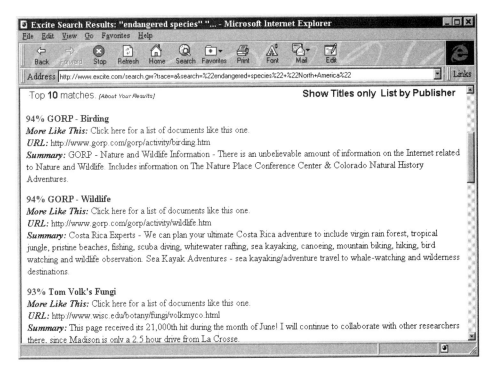

FIGURE 5.3: The results of a search using the search tool called Excite adding to the phrase **"endangered species"** and **"North America"** for the search.

2. Select the right tool to use for your search.

You can use a number of search tools when you are looking for answers. The ones listed in *Common Search Tools* are the most popular, and all do things a little differently. In fact, some of them provide lists of sites that have been reviewed and included in a database. This helps sort out the trash on the Internet from the really good stuff.

Common Search Tools

Yahooligans!	http://www.yahooligans.com
Yahoo!	http://www.yahoo.com
Excite	http://www.excite.com
AltaVista	http://www.altavista.digital.com
Hotbot	http://www.hotbot.com
Infoseek	http://www.infoseek.com
Magellan	http://www.mckinley.com
Lycos	http://www.lycos.com
WebCrawler	http://www.webcrawler.com

Using Categories

Many times it is easier to find answers to your questions by narrowing down categories instead of searching for a specific word or phrase. Most of the popular search engines allow you to search by categories (sports, news, entertainment, and so on). So instead of typing in **"basketball scores"** in the search field of your favorite search engine, you could use the Excite search tool and go from the "Sports" category to the "Basketball" category and have your choice of appropriate sites. It's a little faster and can really help you structure your search. Be sure to check out Yahooligans!, the one created specifically for kids!

Every search tool is a little different, so make sure that you look at any Help available on the screen. The information will usually tell you how to make your search the most effective.

3.

Enter your keyword or phrase and then review the sites that the computer found for your search.

How the search tool returns the sites it finds from your search can be a little different. Look at the results in Figure 5.4 to see the results received when using Magellan.

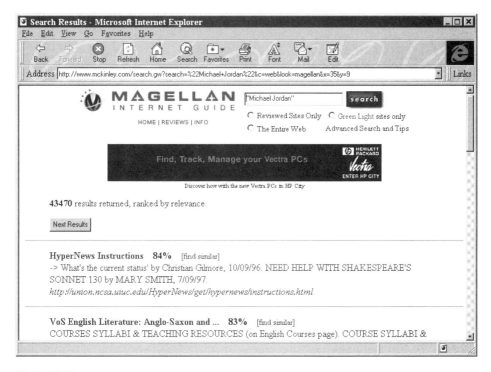

FIGURE 5.4: **Results of searching for "Michael Jordan" from Magellen.**

Now see the results of searching for "**Michael Jordan**" using the search tool Webcrawler (see Figure 5.5).

FIGURE 5.5: Results of searching for **"Michael Jordan"** from WebCrawler.

Oh! Great internetsearch.com, help me find the answer...

Both sites in this example provide percentages that tell you how close the computer thinks the site is to what you are looking for. The closer the site is to the top of the list, the more relevant it is to your search.

Magellan offers a few other options as well. At the top, you can select the boundaries of the search: the entire Web, reviewed sites only, or Green Light sites only. (Green Light sites are those identified as appropriate for young eyes). Magellan also offers a bit of a description of the site providing you with a little bit more information to help you evaluate your choices.

TIP

When you are having difficulty finding what you need, try searching using a variety of tools since they search different collections of sites, and present the results in different ways.

Once you find the titles of a few sites that look interesting to you, click on them to go directly to them. If it doesn't meet your needs, click the Back button or use the Go menu to return to your search results. Keep clicking back and forth until you've got what you need! By doing so, you can go back to the list of search results and select another site until you find the information you need.

4. Create your own personal collection of information.

Several of these search tools let you customize your own page of information so that as soon as you get on the Web, you see current information that is interesting to you. For example, Excite lets you create "My Channel," which is a customized page that can only be accessed by you once you choose a password. You select the information that you want by putting check marks next to the information you want. If you want basketball scores but not football scores, you put a check mark in the box next to basketball (see Figure 5.6).

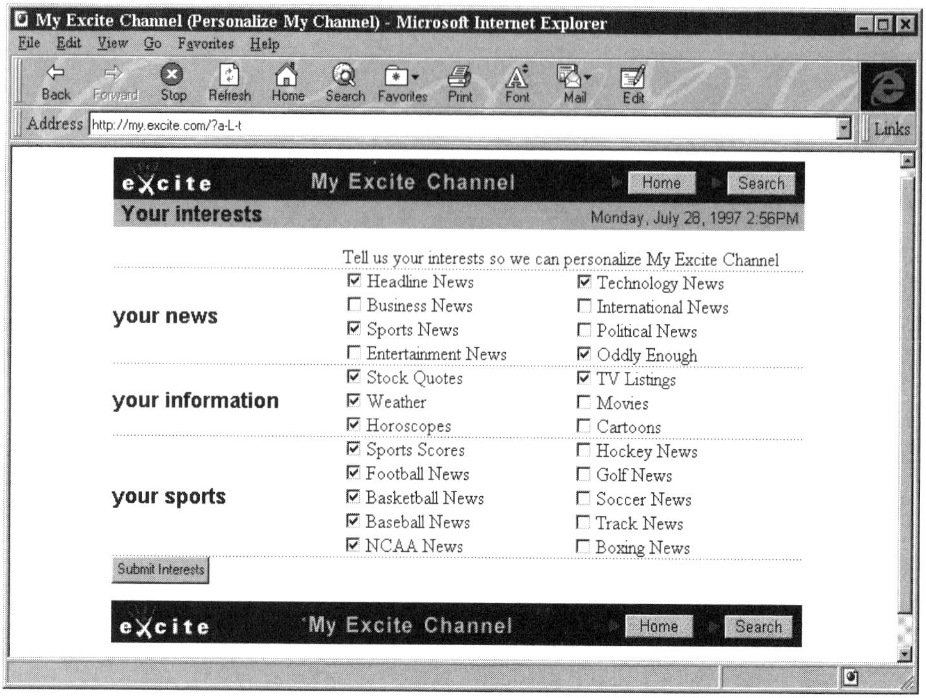

FIGURE 5.6: Customizing "My Channel" in Excite

As you experiment with different search enginges, you will get to know the strengths and limitations of each one. Over time you will develop favorites that you will use again and again.

HOT! HOT! HOT!

My Virtual Reference Desk
http://www.refdesk.com

An amazing collection of reference resources such as the Webster's Dictionary, encyclopedias, atlases, weather, and others in many other subject areas. This site is bound to have a resource that can help you answer you question.

HOT! HOT! HOT!

The Scout Report
http://www.ilhawaii.net/~heinsite/money/scou0809.html

Published every Friday both on the Web and by e-mail, it provides a fast, convenient way to stay informed of valuable resources on the Internet.

K.I.D.S.
http://wwwscout.cs.wisc.edu/scout/KIDS

This is similar to the Scout Report, but it is produced bimonthly by kids, for kids. It is an ongoing, cooperative effort of two classrooms in Boulder, CO and Madison, WI.

PointCast
http://www.redcreek.net/pointcast.htm

This company provides you with free software to download that lets you have your very own news station on the Internet! Throughout the day you can get up-to-the-minute news. (Available for Windows users only.)

Intermind
http://www.intermind.com

When you become a member of Intermind (which is free) you can select the "channels" (Web sites) that you frequent the most and they come up on your own page. You will also be informed when a site is updated with new information.

Writer's Corner

There's a corner of the Internet reserved for all aspiring writers, and it is filled with works by famous authors from ancient to modern times. After reading a few stories, poems, or plays, you may be inspired to take new and different approaches to your own writing.

You're in the middle of writing an exciting adventure story about one of your favorite characters that is caught in a seemingly hopeless situation. You've thought about many things she could do to save herself, but none of them seem just right for your heroine.

One way to jump-start your imagination is to read the writing of other authors. On the Web you will find the works of classic authors such as William Shakespeare, Anne Frank, and Mark Twain as well as contemporary authors like Judy Blume, M.E. Kerr, Virginia Hamilton, and R.L. Stine. There are also works of fiction, poetry, and non-fiction that kids just like you have published on the Internet. Let your mind relax and relive the wild adventures other writers have shared before you put the wheels of your own mind into motion.

Five: Getting the Answer... Now!

The Internet feature you will use in this project is the Web.

There are thousands of stories, novels, and poems on the Web. You can make them your starting point as you begin to write your masterpiece.

1. Find out what works of literature are available through the Internet.

For each of the places listed in *Finding Literature on the Net*, there is an index or catalog of the books and poems you can find at each site. The Web sites listed contain thousands of literary works—more, probably, than your school's library. So get lost in the world of Web lit—happy reading!

read

Finding Literature on the Net

Gutenberg Project
http://promo.net/pg

The Internet Public Library
http://www.ipl.org

The Bartleby Project
http://www.columbia.edu/acis/bartleby

The Internet Poetry Archive
http://sunsite.unc.edu/dykki/poetry/home.html

Poet's Corner
http://pen1.pen.k12.va.us/Anthology/Pav/LangArts/
poetcorner.html

A Celebration of Women Writers
http://almond.srv.cs.cmu.edu/afs/cs.cmu.edu/user/mmbt/
www/women/celebration.html

When you are reading what other kids have written, think about how you could share your work with others on the Web like the project shown in Figure 5.7. Take a look at the cool sites listed in *Web Lit from Kids* for some ideas.

FIGURE 5.7: **In this online project, students from Ann Arbor, Michigan, wrote folk tales set in Africa with online help from volunteers from Nigeria, Egypt, and Kenya.**

Web Lit from Kids

The Inkwell
http://www.geocities.com/SoHo/5249

Too Cool for Grownups
http://www.tcfg.com

2. Pick a story, poem, or play to use as a starting point.

Do you ever wish that a story you are reading would end differently? A fun way to start a story of your own is to write a different version of a work by someone else. You can write a modern version of Shakespeare's *Romeo and Juliet*. You can even write a new ending to a famous book like *Charlotte's Web*—then show it to the world *on* the Web!

Another way to spark your imagination is to take a work of art as your inspiration. For example, you can find a beautiful painting or sculpture on the Web and write about it. If you have questions about what is happening in the work of art ("Why is the Mona Lisa smiling?"), invent answers to them in your writing. Before you know it, you'll be out of your rut and on track toward a great new story!

3. Write your masterpiece.

When you are writing, you might start with an outline of what happens (called the *plot*). With a good outline, you can start writing your story with confidence. Feel free, however, to go back and change your outline if you change your mind about the plot.

If you plan to post your work on the Web for others to read and enjoy, you need to think about the structure of the story as you write it. Will it all be on one page, or will you allow the reader to follow links to several alternate endings? These decisions will affect how you write your story and eventually set up your Web site, so you should sketch out a simple map of your story.

4. Publish it!

Once you have finished writing, you should share it with other writers and readers. It can be a little scary to share your writing, but it is very interesting to hear what people have to say about your story. Each person will find something different and unique based on his or her own experiences.

While you probably won't have big publishing companies waving contracts in your face (at least, not right away…), you can find lots of different ways to help your literary work find an audience. You can read it aloud, act it out with your friends, and print it out on paper to hand it out in your school. Better yet, spare a tree and publish your work the paperless way—on the Web!

To learn how to share your writing through the Internet, try the *Publish It!* project in Chapter 7, which will help you find writing contests you can enter.

Web publishing can be difficult, so stay organized and seek help from your Internet service provider or other experts. After your work "goes live" on the Net, let people know it's there and encourage their feedback. You could even allow your readers to contribute their own stories and additions to your work. Very quickly, you might realize that you are the founder and editor of an online literary magazine!

You're a Writer!

Congratulations! You have not only explored the writing of great writers, tapped the resources of the Internet, but also written your own story.

The Web offers great resources for locating hard-to-find books. If you have a book assigned to you at school, you now know how to get it easily without searching all over town for it. And, as with everything you do on the Internet, you now have a wealth of ideas for your own writing.

Story Starters

Here are a few story starters to get you moving:

★ Write a modern version of a classic work of literature. For example, Greek myths set in the present day.

★ Change the format of a story to read like an exchange of letters between the characters or as various journal entries of either character. You might take Mark Twain's *The Adventures of Tom Sawyer* and create a series of letters between Huck Finn and Tom.

★ Imagine that you could be transported into a story that you really like. What would you do, and what sort of a role would you play? For instance, what would you do if you could go to the magical land of C.S. Lewis' *Narnia* series?

HOT! HOT! HOT!

Bookwire
http://www.bookwire.com

Here you can find lots of stuff on books and their authors.

Classic Short Stories
http://www.bnl.com/shorts

Dedicated to the American short story, this site offers many stories and opportunities to post your own.

Project Eris
gopher://gopher.vt.edu:10010/10/33

If you enjoy reading from your computer screen, this is the gopher site for you, with dozens of classic texts—all in fast-loading, plain-vanilla text.

It's My Thing

What's your thing? What is the one thing you love to do above and beyond everything else? Is it playing a sport like tennis or football? Is it making things like kites or masks? Do you like to collect things such as sports cards, coins, or stamps? Whatever your

don't ask me why

it's just my thing

d-:

hobby, you can find information related to your interests—as well as people who share that interest—on the Internet.

The Internet features used in this project are e-mail, the Web, and listservs.

What do you do when school is out, your home-work is done, and you're ready to kick back and have a good time? Are you a diehard football fan? A horse lover? A cycling nut? Maybe you prefer collecting stamps or autographs, or per-haps your idea of fun is to grab your camera and head out in pursuit of the perfect shot. Regardless of what your interests are, the Internet lets you experience them in ways you never before dreamed possible. You'll find statis-tics and trivia about your favorite hobby...updates on soap operas...your favorite music group's touring schedule—a world of information is at your fingertips. And best of all, you will meet and communicate with others who share your interest.

Pursuing Your Passion

Hobbies are as unique as people; they come in different varieties. You probably have a hobby of your own. Follow these steps to learn how to pursue your hobby on the Internet:

1. Focus on one hobby.

Before you begin pursuing *all* of your interests on the Internet, you may want to narrow down your preferences to just one thing. For example, if you search the Internet for everything that deals with music, you will come up with a list of thousands of Internet sites and resources. Instead, focus your search on the name of a specific group or artist, or maybe one type of music. The same is true if you want information on a sport or television show, be very specific. "The Simpsons" and "Star Trek" are just two of many shows that have their own listservs and multiple fan-supported Web sites. The Internet is also exploding with resources for the sports fan, so be sure to target your main sporting interest. That way you won't have to plow through lists of every sport from archery to volleyball when you want to learn only about soccer.

So you say you don't have a hobby? Or that your hobby is so unusual that surely no one else will share your interests? Take a look at the variety of topics you can explore on the Internet in *Popular Hobbies*—and these aren't the only ones!

Popular Hobbies

Animals	Fishing	Science Fiction
Arts and crafts	Guitars	Scouting
Astronomy	Magic	Scuba diving
Auto racing	Movies and movie stars	Skateboarding
Bagpipe playing	Motorcycles	Snowboarding
Baseball card collecting	Mountain climbing	Spelunking
Building models	Music	Sports
Cooking	Pets	Trains
Dance	Photography	Travel
Dolls	Piano	Video Games
Ferrets	Riding Rollercoasters	Windsurfing

TIP #1

You can even learn about a new hobby on the Internet. Choose an unfamiliar topic, and you will open up a whole new world of fun!

2. Explore the resources.

Finding resources on the Internet can be challenging and fun. Check out the project *I Want to Know...* to get some ideas about creative ways to search the Internet. As you explore, you will run across all kinds of interesting places you will want to go back to later. Bookmark these sites so you won't forget them.

If your hobby is very specialized or unusual, you might have to use a bit of detective work to find resources. Try broadening your search or looking for related hobbies. If you keep coming up with a dead end, ask other users for advice. It's perfectly OK to make mistakes and to ask for help. Other Internet users are usually happy to help you find your way.

You can begin your search with the places listed in *Some Places to Try* even if they do not match your topic (see Figure 5.8). One of the examples is the List of Listservs, which is great place to start communicating with other hobbyists. Through a listserv discussion, you will discover many other resources, online and offline, and share your enthusiasm with other like-minded kids and adults.

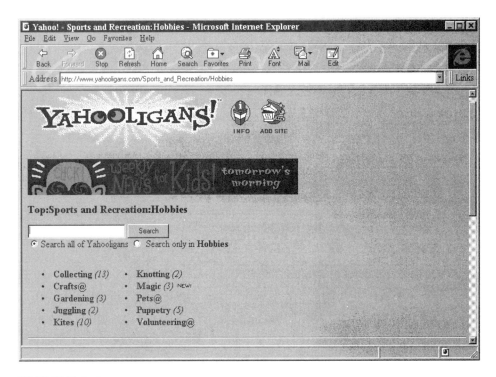

FIGURE 5.8: **Browse the many hobbies listed in Yahooligans!**

Some Places to Try

Yahooligans! Hobbies Index
http://www.yahooligans.com/Sports_and_Recreation/Hobbies

List of Listservs
http://www.NeoSoft.com/internet/pam1/byname.html

CataList
http://www.lsoft.com/lists/list

Fat Cat Cafe
http://fatcatcafe.com/kid/hobby

4. Gather related information.

Now that you are familiar with some of the resources available for your particular area of interest, you can put your Internet skills to work by broadening your knowledge. The more you know about your hobby, the more you will enjoy it and the more you will enjoy sharing information about it on the Internet.

As you learn more about your hobby, you may find that it can become a moneymaker. Many collectors, for example, meet other collectors who are looking for opportunities to buy and sell items. You can research your collectibles over the Internet and consult guides or experts for pricing information.

HOT! HOT! HOT!

Juggling Information Service
http://www.juggling.org

Even jugglers have a site; this one will tell you more
then you ever wanted to know about juggling.

The Birder Home Page
http://www.birder.com

Birds, those singing dinosaurs of the air, make for fascinating study. If you're an expert or a beginner, you'll
enjoy this page.

The Internet Base Camp
http://www.concentric.net/~Foxsfca

Tie in and check out this site, which is packed with
information and has links to other resources.

American Girl
http://www.americangirl.com/ag/ag.cgi

This is an online club for girls with neat ideas, places to
talk, and interesting articles.

Going to Extremes

People, places, and events capture the adventurous side of our imagination. Whether it's the Super Bowl, a trip to the South Pole, a political victory, a historical anniversary, or the biggest concert, everyone can identify an event that fascinates them. With the projects in this chapter, you will learn how to travel through cyber-space—the world of the Internet—to participate in special events:

★ *Virtual Excursions* lets you be a part of expeditions and adventures that other people in the world are leading.

★ *Challenging Contests* demands your best to compete with people all over the world for prizes and recognition of your talents.

★ *The Main Event* connects you to special events happening both on and off the Internet.

With the projects in this chapter, you can be a part of these special events, some of which may even go down in history books!

Virtual Excursions

Are you an adventurer? Do you want to travel the world, braving physical challenges, to find answers to scientific questions? If so, *Virtual Excursions* is the project for you. Through the Internet, you will connect with scientists and other adventurers who are out there right now in the midst of exploration. You can also learn to report on your very own adventures to the world through the Internet.

When most people hear the word "science," they think of people in white coats in laboratories handling glass beakers and Bunsen burners on spotless countertops. However, this is only one vision of science. Some scientists pursue adventurous, and sometimes dangerous, expeditions that take them into previously unexplored territory. Like Indiana Jones, they go to the tops of mountains, across deserts and tundra, and through jungles to find answers to questions they have about how the world works.

Although laboratories provide controlled environments for experiments, not every scientific question can be answered in a lab. This is why some scientists go on expeditions to collect data and samples from the field. For instance, if an Alaskan scientist is trying to figure out why the antelope population is declining in the Alaskan interior, the answer can only be found by going out into the wilderness and observing the behavior of the antelopes; this is called *field research*.

Scientists doing field research often face interesting challenges. They may have to learn how to be prepared campers, how to survive in extreme weather conditions, and how to transport the data they have collected safely back to their laboratories.

Now that you know a few general facts about scientific expeditions, follow the steps in this project to get connected to a real scientific expedition happening right now. Better yet, organize your own! In any case, make yours a journey of scientific discovery.

The Internet features you will use for this project are e-mail, listservs, and the Web.

Joining the Expedition

The only ticket you need for an expedition is a connection to the Internet. Once you are connected and online, though, you'll have to make up your mind about where you want to go and what you hope to learn.

1. Decide which virtual expedition you want to join.

Before you join an online adventure, you need to know where people are going and why. A good place to start is with the Web sites listed in *Virtual Journeys*. As you can see in Figure 6.1, you could be part of the Discovery Channel by clicking on their Exploration link.

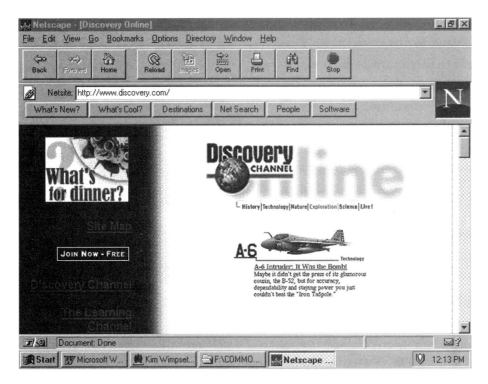

FIGURE 6.1: **Check out the Discovery Channel's Web Site to join an online adventure** (http://www.discovery.com).

Virtual Journeys

Virtual Voyager
http://www.chron.com/voyager/index.html

Travel to the depths of the oceans or to the heights of outer space.

MayaQuest
http://www.mecc.com/mayaquest.html

Explore the jungles of Central America looking for clues to the lost civilization of the Maya. Your participation in the expedition is encouraged!

Virtual Journeys (cont.)

Discovery Channel Online: Exploration
`http://www.discovery.com`

With expeditions going on all the time, Discovery brings you along on expeditions in search of dinosaurs, elephants, sharks, and much more.

2. Learn about the scientists' mission.

After you have selected an expedition to follow, collect information and learn more about it. Each expedition will have a unique purpose. Find out why the scientists are working in a particular part of the world. Many times you can find background information about the mission, the type of research, and the scientific team, as well as how you can participate in the expedition right on their Web site.

Every project will be designed a little bit differently. Some people will create a listserv that they will use to distribute messages from the field, background materials, and questions from subscribers. Most projects will establish a Web site to organize all of the information and communication. Because each situation is different, pay close attention to the instructions you receive when you sign up to participate.

3. Ask questions.

As you read the background information and updates from the scientists in the field, develop questions to help yourself better understand what is happening. In many of these projects, your questions for the scientists are welcome. Be as specific and detailed as you can so the scientists can fully answer your questions. *The JASON Project* is one example.

The JASON Project

This project was started by the scientist who discovered the Titanic, Dr. Robert D. Ballard, because he received so many letters from students asking how he made his discovery. Each year students around the country join scientists on a variety of adventures through computer communication and satellite links.

One of the recent JASON Project expeditions was a trip to the country of Belize in Central America to examine the health of planet Earth by studying a rainforest and the largest barrier reef in the Western Hemisphere.

The best part is that you are invited to participate—check out the JASON Project at http://www.jasonproject.org **(see Figure 6.2).**

4.   Be a good team member.

Sharing scientific adventure online can be more than a passing spectacle if you are willing to work. If you take every opportunity to participate in and support the expedition, you will have more fun and certainly learn more.

In one adventure to Antarctica, for example, a small plane carrying several members of the team and a great deal of equipment crashed in Chile, a country on the west side of South America. Thankfully, there were just a few minor injuries. However, the equipment was destroyed. Without more money, the expedition would have ended. When students heard about this, they collected money from local communities to help the scientists continue their work. Instantly they became part of the team.

Always remember that you are dealing with real human beings—not TV characters—so treat them with respect.

FIGURE 6.2: **Connect with other kids and get involved with the JASON Project** (http://www.jasonproject.org).

You Can Be the Virtual Travel Agent

1. Plan a local expedition.

The best way to understand the purpose of scientific expeditions, besides participating in them online, is to organize one yourself. What is unique about where you

live? Are there special plants or animals? Are you near the mountains or the sea? Answering these questions will help you create a scientific question that you and your friends can research. For instance, if you live by the sea, you might want to explore nearby beaches for fascinating marine life like sea turtles.

2. Invite others to join your trip...virtually.

If you are going on a scientific expedition, a great way to get the word out is to post information about your trip to one of the listservs described in *Kids' Listservs*. You will need to post the information well in advance of the trip date so other people will have enough time to send you questions before you go. Look at *Posting Field Trip Information* for a simple way to submit your field trip information.

TIP

When you talk about your trip be sure to keep the details of where you are staying or other personal information private. Your Internet friends would love to know about the sites you see and things you learn.

Kids' Listservs

Kidlink
http://www.kidlink.org/

Kidsphere
subscribe to kidsphere@vms.cis.pitt.edu

There are a variety of Usenet groups like k12.ed.math, k12.ed.science, k12.ed.art, **and so on. Check with your ISP to determine which K12 groups are available to you.**

Invite the other kids you meet through the listserv or Usenet group to help you with your scientific expedition. They can participate by sending you e-mail with questions, observations, or ideas that they may have about your expedition. You can also post an announcement on the Web.

Use input from others to help you formulate a scientific research question. Your research question will be the thing that expedition is trying to answer. An example would be "How long does it take for a Loggerhead Sea Turtle to hatch from its egg?" What's great about this is that not everyone lives near a Loggerhead Sea Turtle habitat, but maybe you do. You get to be the scientist on the expedition, and, using the Internet, you can bring people to learn about what's unique in your backyard!

Also, you can collect all sorts of questions (like, "How far from the water do they nest?") from your virtual companions on the Net; you will be able to investigate when you reach your destination and then share your findings.

Posting Field Trip Information

Your full name:

Your e-mail address:

Grade:

Subject of class (math, science, etc.):

Where is your excursion destination?

What are the dates of your visit?

Describe the kinds of things you will see on your trip and what you think you might learn from the excursion.

What help from others do you need in order to complete the expedition?

3. Take your research trip.

Once you have a question, plan an expedition to observe and collect data. Think about the supplies you'll need for your trip (no matter how short) and how you will collect the information you need to answer your question.

Then hit the road, Jack.

When you are answering the questions sent to you by other kids on the Internet, try to respond as completely as possible. You are their eyes on the trip, so be as descriptive as possible. For example, you could write, "The Statue of Liberty is on an island," but it would be more descriptive and interesting to write: "The Statue of Liberty is on Liberty Island in New York Harbor, southwest of Manhattan Island. She is 151 ft. (46m) high from the base she stands on to the top of the torch in her uplifted right hand. Her dress is draped like an ancient Roman toga; she also wears a crown and holds a book with the inscription 'July 4, 1776.'" You get the idea…and don't forget to have fun!

Hopefully, you were able to answer your scientific question through your work on your expedition. If not, think about changing your question or gathering different data. Many times scientists have to go on four or five expeditions before they find an answer. All scientists have one thing in common: They never stop searching for answers.

4. Share your discoveries with the world.

Besides the kids you have contacted through the Internet, there are probably other people in your community who would be interested in learning about your virtual field trip. Think of unique ways that you could share your questions and answers with others. Maybe this is a great school project. Maybe your local newspaper would like you to write a guest editorial describing your experiences. You could also create a computer presentation using pictures, graphics, sound, and even digital movies to show what you learned (see *Keep a Log or Journal*).Or create a Web site featuring all of these elements (see Chapter 9 for help designing and building your Web site).

Keep a Log or Journal

All scientists keep a log or journal filled with descriptions of their observations. While something may seem insignificant at the time, a week later it may help answer a key question. Your notes will become very valuable for you, so keep them in a safe place, away from damaging elements like water.

HOT! HOT! HOT!

The Adventure WebRing
http://www.realkids.com/webring.htm

The WebRing links together lots of terrific tales of adventure, travel, and discovery.

Kidlink
http://www.kidlink.org/KIDLINK

Kidlink is a project to get kids aged 10-15 involved in a global dialog, through a fun Web site, activities, and a newsletter.

HOT! HOT! HOT!

CoVis: Learning through Collaborative Visualization
http://www.covis.nwu.edu

Here you can check out scientists sharing information and expertise on the Internet.

Global Online Adventure Learning Site (GOALS)
http://www.adventureonline.com/other/goals.html

Dedicated to online learning, GOALS is also full of the spirit of adventure on such trips as a rowing expedition trying to make it around the world and three young brothers on a two-year sailing trip around the Pacific Ocean.

Challenging Contests

In *Challenging Contests*, you will find and participate in contests of all kinds. If you like to cook, enter a recipe contest. If you like to paint, enter a fridge art contest. Since the Internet is global, you'll be competing with people all over the world and maybe even winning a prize!

Five intertwined rings symbolize the greatest contest in the world: the Olympic Games. Every two years there is either a summer games or winter games where many athletes' dreams come true. The Olympics provides the ultimate contest—one where training, determination, luck, and energy come together to produce Olympic champions.

The Olympic Games is a collection of contests that test athletes' physical abilities and skills. But there are thousands of other contests in the world that test other areas, such as writing, acting, painting, building, problem solving, and others. With the Internet you can now find contests to enter and compete for almost anything you enjoy doing.

The Internet features you will use for this project are e-mail, listservs, and the Web.

You're the Next Contestant On...

The word "contestant" refers to a person participating in a contest, which is the root of the word. You usually hear the word "contestant" on television game shows and the word "competitor" at athletic events, but they pretty much mean same thing. Regardless of what you are called during the contest, you always become a winner by participating in an event, because you challenge yourself by competing. Follow these steps to find the right contest for you.

1. Use the Internet to find out about contests.

Many contest organizers post notices of upcoming contests on the Internet so the information will get to a large number of people in a variety of geographic areas. There are several different approaches to finding contests on the Internet.

The quickest way to get a list of Internet-posted contests is to go through a category search for contests. Yahooligans! is one search tool that actually has a category called "Contests," which is part of the larger category called "Entertainment." When you bring up this page, you should see something similar to Figure 6.3, although the sites may have changed over time.

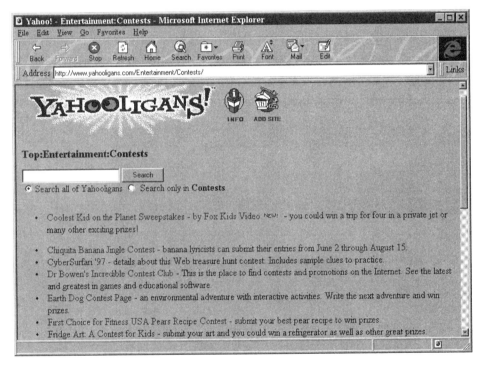

FIGURE 6.3: **In the Entertainment category of Yahooligans!, you can get a list of contests ranging from art to writing to collaborative thinking.**

Since many companies have Web sites, they often use contests to attract visitors...especially those companies that make products or provide services for young people. For instance, one of the contests listed in Figure 6.3 is the Chiquita Banana Jingle Contest where kids can submit their lyrics for a new song to use in a commercial.

There are also organizations such as National Aeronautics Space Association (NASA) that sponsor contests occasionally that deal with a particular subject area like space. (NASA Spacelink is at `http://spacelink.nasa.gov`.) Check *Where to Search for a Contest* for a few places to begin your search.

Where to Search for a Contest

Yahooligans!
Use your Web browser to go to `http://www.yahooligans.com` **and look for "Contests" in the "Entertainment" category.**

Dr. Bowen's Incredible Contest Club
Go to `http://www.contestclub.com`

WWW 4 kidz Weekly Contests
Go to `http://www.4kidz.com`

Several contests are held on a regular basis so even if you missed the deadline this year, you can create your battleplan for next year or the next deadline. Investigate the contests listed in *Ongoing Contests* to see which one appeals to you. (The one in Figure 6.4 claims that the awards can total more than $1 million dollars!) The one thing to remember with regular contests is that each year more and more contestants enter making the competition stiff…but not impossible!

Ongoing Contests

CyberSurfari http://www.spa.org/cybersurfari

ThinkQuest http://www.advanced.org/thinkquest

**Visa Olympics of the Imagination
WWW to** http://www.visa.com/cgi-bin/vec/ev/
voi/main.html?2+0 **and then click on "Special
Events."**

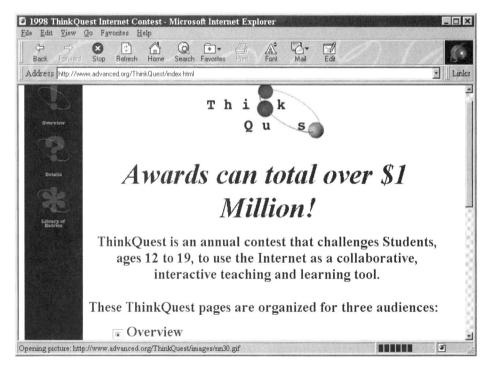

FIGURE 6.4: ThinkQuest challenges students, ages 12 to
19, to use the Internet as a collaborative,
interactive teaching and learning tool.

2. Read the requirements of the contest (the fine print!).

One of the keys to winning a contest is to find out exactly what the judges are looking for. In addition to the contest deadline, there may be other rules you need to know, such as:

★ Registration procedures

★ Submission formats

★ Contest deadlines

Challenge yourself. Try something new. You may be the winner of the next Internet contest.

3. Enter the contest.

Once you find a contest that you want to enter, plan your strategy. For instance, read the Earth Dog Contest posting (see Figure 6.5). Now you might make the following plan:

1. Read through each environmental problem by Oct. 1.

2. Read three essays written by different authors by Oct. 10.

3. Write a first draft of my own essay by Oct. 22.

4. Ask two people whose writing I respect to review my essay by Oct. 31.

5. Make revisions and type up the final draft of my essay by Nov. 15.

6. Submit my essay (and any additional information required) to the contest by the deadline: Nov. 30.

Notice this sample plan includes dates that are mini-deadlines. By making these, you help yourself plan ahead.

FIGURE 6.5: **Announcement and Rules for the Earth Dog Contest is an example of how important it is to read the rules and know the deadline!**

Here Comes the Judge

In this activity, you can be the judge by creating your own contest and offering prizes or recognition. Maybe you are interested in space travel. What kind of contest based on this topic might be interesting? Perhaps something like the Space Station Contest, which asks people to submit designs for a research station in space, would be intriguing. Check *Contest Ideas* for suggestions of contests you might want to sponsor.

Create Your Own Contest

You can sponsor your own contest with a little planning and creativity. Decide on contest requirements *before* you invite people to participate. Here are some questions to ask yourself:

★ What is the topic?

★ What do you want people to submit?

★ What is the deadline?

★ If you are collecting written responses, is there a limit to how long they can be?

★ If people are searching for answers to specific questions, how will they get access to the questions at the same time and in a fair way?

★ How will the entries be evaluated and who will judge them?

★ What will the winners receive…recognition or a prize?

Before you post anything on the Internet, try the contest out on your friends. This way, you can check to make sure you've included all the steps. Check *Listservs and Usenet Groups for Posting Your Contest* for places to post your contest.

Contest Ideas

➤ Create a set of crossword puzzles or word games for people to solve.

➤ Ask for skits written about a historical or current situation and judge them on how humorous and creative they are.

➤ Collect short science fiction stories and choose the best based on the creativity of the story and the logic of the author's predictions.

➤ Hold a competition for computer-designed artwork.

Listservs and Usenet Groups for Posting Your Contest

KIDLINK
WWW to `http://www.kidlink.org,` **which has guides to help you subscribe to** `listserv@listserv.nodak.edu.`

KIDLINK
Find great Usenet groups at
`http://www.worldkids.net/kotw/mail.htm.`

When you subscribe to a listserv, you are adding yourself to a list of e-mail recipients. When you post a message on a listserv, you are sending an e-mail message to everyone else who has subscribed to the list.

Prizes and Recognition

Everyone loves competing for a prize even if you aren't offering cars, diamonds, or free trips! Think about what would be meaningful to your contest participants. For example, one of the prizes for winners of the now-defunct Internet scavenger hunt was a free subscription to an Internet magazine. It is pretty certain that anyone entering an Internet contest will enjoy a prize like this one. Or maybe you want to create recognition certificates to send across the network. Perhaps you'll find you have as much fun competing in contests as in creating them.

HOT! HOT! HOT!

First Step to Nobel Prize in Physics
http://www.almaz.com/nobel

The Noble Prize Internet Archive sponsors this international physics research paper competition for high school students.

Freezone
http://freezone.com

This is a wild site with lots of fun stuff to do including contests that you can win!

Acekids
http://www.acekids.com/games.html

The Academic Center for Excellence (ACE) sponsors several contests such as brain teasers and poetry writing.

Kids' Place in Space
http://www.vsv.com/kidship/index.html

Sponsored by Virgin Entertainment, this site offers a monthly contest and gives out free software to winners!

The Main Event

What big events capture your imagination? The Super Bowl? The Oscar awards? Presidential elections? The probe landing on Mars? People all over the world eagerly follow these and many other events. The Internet is a great tool that lets you obtain information and talk to people before, during, and after *The Main Event*. For many of these big events, people create online resources for background information, daily or hourly updates, and connections to people who are just as captivated as you.

You have read all the magazine articles, you have watched all the preview television shows, you have seen all the nominated films—you are fully prepared for an evening at the Oscars. It is going to be a long night in front of the television, so you have a stock of snacks and sodas ready to go. Some people might say you are obsessed with the Oscars, but you look forward to the event all year because you enjoy movies and dream of becoming a famous director. The Oscars help you learn the ropes of the profession and the secrets of film style.

Sound familiar? If not, maybe you look forward to a different kind of big event—sports championships or musical concerts—but chances are it is related to a favorite hobby that you may have explored in the *It's My Thing* project in Chapter 5. You may be a big fan of the people who are well-known and successful in your area of interest.

Fans are very important. They show support, they share their enthusiasm, and they help attract more people to the event. This project offers you new ways to express your "fanatical" feelings and meet others who share them.

Your Connection to the Big Events

In practically every month of the year, some kind of big event is happening somewhere in the world. While you may only know about those that happen in America, such as the Grammy awards for music, important events happen all around the world. For example, soccer's World Cup takes place in a different country every four years with teams from many different countries competing to be the best in the world. Another main event occurred in South Africa when Nelson Mandela became South Africa's first black president—a stunning achievement for a country that for so long supported the policy of apartheid, which discriminates against people of color. His inauguration was televised around the world.

You can tune into current world events by following these steps.

1. Find an upcoming event that interests you.

You will want to find an event that is happening in the near future. The nearer in time the event is, the more attention in the media and on the Internet there will be. Obviously, newspapers, magazines, and television are good sources of articles that preview upcoming events.

Many events are seasonal, such as the Super Bowl, which always happens in January. Spring signals spring training for baseball. Summer brings musical concert tours. Fall is election time. Think about what season it is now and what events are typical of the season. *Big Events in the World* will provide you with more event ideas.

Big Events in the World

Space Shuttle Launch (throughout the year)
http://spacelink.nasa.gov

Nobel Prize Awards (early October)
http://www.almaz.com/nobel

Wimbledon Tennis Championships (June)
http://www.wimbledon.org

Earth Day (April)
http://www.envirolink.org/earthday

The Grammy Music Awards (March)
http://www.grammy.com

The Iditarod Dog Sled Race (March)
http://www.iditarod.org

National Basketball Association's Championships (May)
http://www.nba.com

Women's National Basketball Championships (August)
http://www.wnba.com

2. Locate information about the event and find other people who are interested in it.

Once you have chosen an event to explore on the Internet, look for resources that were created only for that event, as well as for permanent

sites that include a variety of special event resources. Check in *Special Event Information* for the addresses of the permanent sites. Many times notices of event activities on the Internet will be posted on listservs related to the subject of the event, such as politics, sports, science, literature, and others.

Special Event Information

The Scout Report
http://scout.cs.wisc.edu/scout/report

This report offers a regular update of all new sites and resources on the Internet.

Yahooligans!
http://www.yahooligans.com

This site provides a category "The Scoop" that includes the category "Current Events."

If you subscribe to the Scout Report—a weekly report sent to you through electronic mail—it will inform you of the newest sites on the Internet that may focus on an upcoming event. The report includes listservs, Web pages, new menu items on a Gopher, or even a new Telnet site.

If you are at a loss for where to look for information about an event, search the Web for your topic. Chances are the sites you find will have additional links to related sites as well.

3. Check for daily updates.

Once you locate a resource, bookmark the address (see how to do this in Chapter 1), and write down any log-in instructions. You will want to consult these resources before, during, and after the event for all kinds of updated information. If you have subscribed to a listserv, there will be new messages from other Internet users.

There are also now *live* events on the Internet. In particular, many radio stations broadcast on the Internet as well as to radios where they are located. How do you find out about these broadcasts? Many of the search tools (see Chapter 5) provide daily updates like the listing of Net Events from Yahoo! (see Figure 6.6).

Through some of these resources, you have a chance to share your opinions and feelings about what is happening with people who care about the event as much as you do. If the winner of a sports event is a surprise to everyone, share your theory about why that happened on a listserv. If you absolutely loved a new blockbuster movie, tell people why. You will probably get some interesting responses to your opinions. You may want to track results of sporting events or election results and share them in a report at school. You can enhance the facts with the opinions you and your online *correspondents*—the people you communicate with—have shared about the event.

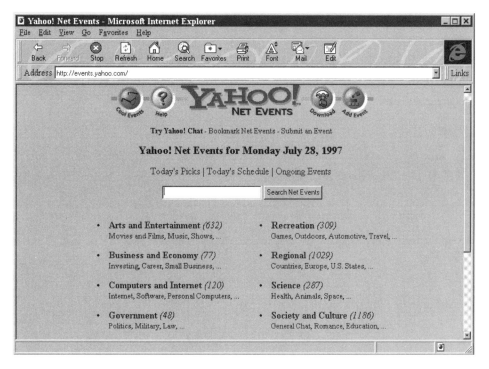

FIGURE 6.6: **At the Yahoo! site, you can get a listing of Net Events and Picks of the Day at** `http://www.yahoo.com.`

HOT! HOT! HOT!

The Oscars
http://www.oscars.org/ampas

Want to know the nominations and winners of the Academy Awards? Go to the official site of the Academy of Motion Picture Arts & Sciences.

ClariNet
http://www.clarinet.com/single/internet.html

ClariNet provides the broadest, up-to-the-minute news coverage on the Internet, with more than 3,500 stories per day from major news wires and continuous updates around the clock.

Intellicast
http://www.intellicast.com

If you want to know about weather events, this is the place to go.

Sharing Your Ideas

How do you tell the world about your great ideas? Maybe you've thought of getting them published in a book or a magazine, recorded onto a CD, shown in an art gallery, or broadcast on the news. The Internet offers all kinds of electronic journals, magazines, galleries, and news services, so you can display your creations far easier than ever before. The projects in this chapter will help you discover the different ways your work can reach the world:

★ *Networked News* connects you to all sorts of youth-oriented news sites on the Web and gives you ideas for creating your very own news site.

★ *Musical Outlets* gives you ideas for what to do with the songs you compose in your head and lets you know where you can find Web sites about music.

★ *The Zine Zone* shows you how to make your own electronic magazine (*zine*) that showcases your writing or poetry.

Networked News

Every night around 5 or 6 P.M., you can watch at least one hour of news on television. Approximately every 60 seconds, a news anchor describes a different event. Ever wonder how these news anchors and television news agencies know about the events that are happening? Or how newspaper reporters find information about the stories they cover?

Most news agencies have several news *bureaus* (offices) scattered around their area of interest—a city, a state, a country, or even the world. These bureaus have a news *staff*, or a collection of employees, that monitors the events in their area and sends reports to the main news agency.

If you contribute to your school's newspaper, you already belong to a news bureau. In addition to putting out the news on paper—hence the word "newspaper"—your bureau could put out the news on the Web (would that make it a "newsweb"?). If you aren't part of your school's newspaper, why not create your own bureau with a group of friends?

The News Bureau

Although a news bureau can include hundreds of people, you can create one with only one person: yourself. Or, if you happen to have some friends who want to form a news bureau, invite them to participate as well. The bureau can be as big or small as you like. (The advantage to having more people is that you can cover more stories.)

1. Decide which jobs everyone wants.

A news bureau has three basic jobs: editor-in-chief, reporter, and copy editor. The editor-in-chief decides which stories are newsworthy and meet the guidelines of the news agency. The reporter researches and writes the story. The copy editor reads the stories to correct spelling and grammatical errors and to make sure that the writing is understandable.

If you are the only person in the bureau, then your choice is easy. You do every job: You decide which stories to cover, you write the stories, and you edit them. If you are working with a team of friends, you and your friends can decide which roles each of you really wants to have. You can figure out which jobs you like by trading roles from time to time.

You can team up with friends in your local area or, for a more national or international flavor, invite friends in other areas of the world to contribute stories or act as editors.

2. Create the focus and content for your news site.

If you are going to make an online version of your school's newspaper, you already have the information you need. The focus is your school community, and the content includes stories and pictures about happenings in your school.

If you are going to create a news site on the Web, you need to think about the intention of the site. That is, what is the purpose of the news site and what will the stories be like? A news site with stories about local bands in Seattle, Houston, and Atlanta would make for interesting comparisons. Or, you could focus on community service projects that kids from around the country have set up. Check out the KidsCare site at http://kidscare.org/ to see an online newsletter in action.

Focus

Take a look at the magazine racks in a local store, and you will quickly realize the wide range of focuses your news site can have—news about local youth, music, fashion, politics, and even animals.

Stories

Will you be writing the stories? Will they be investigative or humorous? Maybe you will put together a collection of interviews of local heroes, or cover the results of your home sports teams.

While you are thinking about these questions, look at some of the sample sites listed in *Youth News Outlets.* Figure 7.1 shows an example of a school newspaper on the Web.

Youth News Outlets

KidNews
http://www.kidnews.com

This is an online news and writing service for students and teachers around the world. Anyone may use stories from the service for educational purposes, and anyone may submit stories.

United Nations Youth Information Network
http://www.un.org/dpcsd/dspd/unyin.htm

The Youth Information Network is a project of the United Nations that tracks issues related to youth around the world.

Jr. Seahawk News
http://www.halcyon.com/arborhts/jrseahaw.html

This site shows one middle school's approach to putting their newspaper on the Web.

Youth News Outlets (cont.)

Aboriginal Youth Network, News Center
http://ayn-0.ayn.ca/PAGES/news.htm

In Australia, many kids are from the aboriginal (or native) tribes. This is a place where news affecting their lives is collected and available.

GLC Online!
http://www.geocities.com/Athens/4582/glc01.html

This newsletter is created by the youth of Loraine, IL and includes stories, polls, and poetry.

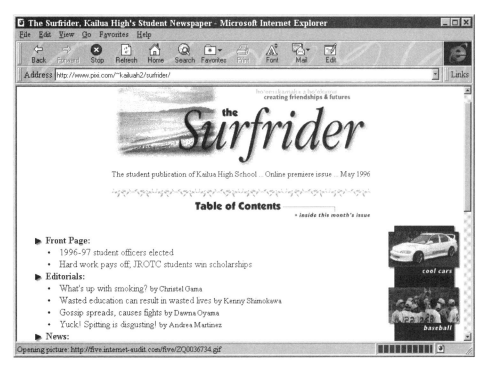

FIGURE 7.1: **The Surfrider is a great example of bringing a school's newspaper on the Web** (http://www.pixi.com/~kailuah2/surfrider).

3. Set a schedule for publishing new issues.

Local newspapers come out every day. Magazines tend to be published weekly or monthly. Many newsletters are published quarterly. Often these publishing cycles are based on the time it takes to actually print the paper version of the issue. With the Web, the time it takes to publish is the time it takes you to put your text, images, photos, and anything else into Web format.

You can create a list of story assignments and submission deadlines to keep focused. If you are working with a team of journalists, you will need to include several mini-deadlines so that the copy editor and the editor-in-chief have time to read and edit the story. If you are working on your own, leave yourself some extra time to double-check your story before putting it up at your site. Chapter 9, "Building Cool Sites on the Web," includes projects that help you build your own Web site step by step. Waiting until the night before the due date often gets the creative juices flowing, but this strategy may not produce a well-written story.

It's also a good idea to read other news articles to analyze writing styles and story ideas. Several newspapers make their articles available over the Internet. Check one of those listed in *Newspapers and Magazines on the Net*. Figure 7.2 shows the main menu of *USA Today*.

Newspaper and Magazines on the Net

Pathfinder
`http://www.pathfinder.com/kids.`

This is the Web site for Time Warner, the publisher of magazines such as *Sports Illustrated*, *Time*, and *Entertainment Weekly*.

Newspaper and Magazines on the Net (cont.)

The Irish Times
http://www.irish-times.ie/.

Get all the latest news and weather across Ireland.

USA Today
http://www.usatoday.com/usafront.htm.

Look here for the Web version of this popular U.S. daily newspaper.

InfiNet newsstand
http://www.infi.net/newsstand.html.

At this Web site you can find an online newspaper among the many that InfiNet operates around the country.

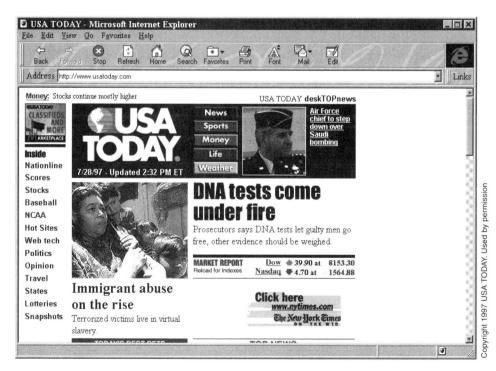

FIGURE 7.2: **USA Today** is one of many newspapers available online.

4. Build your news site.

You've got your news bureau staff working, you know your deadlines, and you are surveying other news stories. Now it's time to create your own news site on the Web. Publishing on the Web is not difficult to learn, but it does take some time. Make sure you consult Chapter 1 and the projects in Chapter 9 to help you acquire the tools and build the skills you will need to do this.

Once you get your news site up and running, be sure you update it regularly. Visitors like to depend on sites that are maintained and updated regularly and that live up to the promises they make. Your readers are interested in reading about what's happening today or this week, not old stuff.

By putting your news bureau on the Web, people on the other side of the planet will get a glimpse into the lives and thoughts of young people in your area.

HOT! HOT! HOT!

Top News
http://www.topnews.com

This is a service of Lycos, a popular search tool, that provides a great array of top news stories every day.

Children's Express
http://www.ce.org

This site is a news service produced by kids reporting on issues that affect their lives.

Afro-American Newspapers
http://www.afroam.org

Every week, this site compiles the top news stories affecting African-Americans across the country.

Musical Outlets

Whether you like rock, rap, hip hop, jazz, funk, or classical music, the Internet is a great place to find musical discussions, resources, and even sound files of musical recordings. While the *Musical Outlets* project will get you in touch with these musical sites, composing a new number-one hit is up to you.

Do you hear music when you daydream? Do you tap your pencils against the table? Are you ever seen *without* a Walkman on your head? If you fit this description, use this project to develop your talent as a musician. Take small steps toward composing your own song with help from other musicians and musical resources on the Internet.

Writing original songs is a creative process similar to writing a story or painting a picture. It takes a combination of talent, motivation, and skill. You can't be taught talent or motivation, but you can learn certain skills that will give you new ways of applying your creative ideas.

As a composer, you decide the tempo of the song, the instruments to be used, and even the lyrics. Composing a song may seem like something you could never do and a little overwhelming. However, you don't have to be a music whiz to do it. As you go through the steps of this project, just have fun and if you take it one piece at a time, you might end up with a great original song.

The Internet features you will use for this project are e-mail, listservs, Usenet, and the Web.

Composing an Original Song

If you talk to a group of songwriters, each person in the group will describe a different technique for writing an original song. Some may wake up in the middle of the night with an inspiration and write an entire song in one hour. Others may start with a few bars of music and slowly complete a song. The following steps provide you with suggestions for exploring the process of writing a song. Using these resources, you can find your own special way of putting it all together.

1. Study your favorite music.

Begin by listening closely to your favorite musical compositions; this will give you a better understanding of your musical preferences. Look at them from different perspectives by asking yourself questions like:

MUSIC NOTES
The WebHeads' new CD offers some awesome melodies, but we find the lyrics a bit stale I mean, hasn t *Yeah, yeah, yeah* been done already, like definitively, by the Beatles?

★ How does it begin? Why does it make me want to listen?

★ What is the primary instrument? What are the supporting instruments?

★ Is there a major, abrupt change, or does the volume or intensity slowly increase or decrease?

★ Does it make me want to dance or close my eyes and dream?

Worldwide Internet Music Resources

This site is your ticket to finding all kinds of musical information. Everything from links to sites for specific artists, to sites about different types of music, to links for musical journals and magazines.

Open your Web browser and go to `http://www.music.indiana.edu/music_resources` **to find all this cool stuff about music.**

The William and Gayle Cook Music Library, on the Indiana University Web site, supports a large music archive in which you can find all kinds of information about thousands of songs by hundred of artists (see *Worldwide Internet Music Resources* for how to get there). Use this archive to collect information about some of your favorite songs and musicians. Figure 7.3 shows you the main menu for this archive.

If you don't already know how to read music, you can try to learn by listening to a song as you follow along on the sheet music. However, it may be faster to learn from someone who knows how to read music for a particular instrument. Check with a local music store or the music teacher at school for information on classes or private lessons.

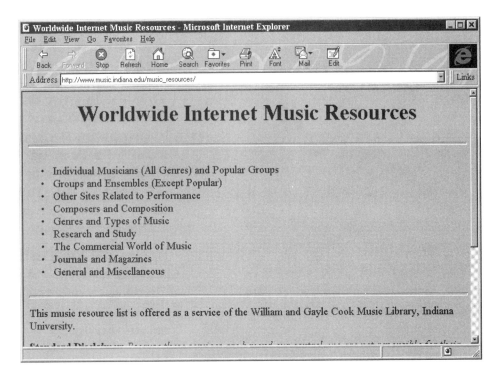

FIGURE 7.3: **Here's what you'll find when you begin to explore the Worldwide Internet Music Resources.** (`http://www.music.indiana.edu/music_resources`).

2. Identify the features of different musical instruments.

As a composer, it helps to understand the design and special qualities of different instruments; it is the harmony of the instruments that gives a composition a distinctive and appealing sound. As you can see from the list of Internet sites in *Instrument Resources*, you can go to several different sites to learn about almost any instrument.

If you don't see it in the list, be sure to check the List of Music Mailing Lists found in *Music Discussion Groups*. By subscribing to one listserv and following the discussion for one week, you will learn more than you can imagine. For example, one of the sites offers guitar *tablatures* for many songs. Tablature is a system of musical notation used most often for stringed instruments. The lines represent the strings, and the notes or letters on them represent finger placement. You can follow the tablature as you listen to the composition. This will help you learn how to play the piece on a guitar.

Instrument Resources

America's Shrine to Music Museum
http://www.usd.edu.smm

This site takes you on a virtual tour of a South Dakota museum, which houses more than 6,000 instruments from all over the world.

The Piano Education Page
http://www.unm.edu/~loritaf/pnoedmn.html

You'll find tips on learning to play the piano, getting the right kind of piano lessons and piano teacher, piano-teaching software, links to other piano and music-related sites, interviews, and a special page for kids.

Guitar Instruction
http://www.scott.net/~mwarren/noframes/instruction.html

You can find everything you want to know about playing the guitar here. This site even includes an online guitar lesson.

Music Discussion Groups

Allmusic

Subscribe to `listserv@american.edu`. **This listserv offers discussion on all forms of music. Topics include composition, musicology, jazz, classical, funk, acoustics, and performance.**

Rec.music.compose

This Usenet group features discussions about notation and composition software, sources of inspiration, getting published, book reviews, and computer hardware used in composition.

Percussion Talk

To join, send e-mail to `rec.music.makers.percussion`. **This is a Usenet group with discussions about percussion instruments.**

List of Music Mailing Lists

`http://www.shadow.net/~mwaas/lomml.html`

Visit this site for a huge list of discussion groups for specific artists or general music topics.

3. Read the lyrics for several different songs.

Find the lyrics to a few of your favorite songs in the Lyrics Library (the address is in *Lyrical Resources*). You will see that the lyrics are actually poems. Sometimes it's easier to think about writing a poem in *stanzas*, or verses, than writing a song's words and music all at once. See if this works for you.

Have an online conversation with someone or a group of people interested in *a cappella* music. This is music where the only instruments used are voices. In addition to words, singers will often make unique sounds or sing nonsensical words, called *scatting*, in an effort to create the illusion of many instruments.

Lyrical Resources

Newsgroup
`Rec.music.a-cappella`

A Usenet group for those who enjoy performing or listening to a cappella (voice-only) music.

The Lyrics Library
`http://web2.kw.igs.net/~wgarvin.lyrics.welcome.html`

This site provides all kinds of lyrical resources.

`Alt.music.lyrics`

A Usenet group for songwriters and anyone else interested in discussing song lyrics.

4. Put your own ideas for instruments and lyrics together to create new melodies.

During your research of different songs, instruments, and lyrics, you may have developed a few ideas of your own. Begin by combining a lyric idea with a few bars of musical notes. Start small—just a bar or two. Then keep adding to your song.

Many musicians are using electronic systems, called MIDIs, to create music. A MIDI system is a lot like a synthesizer, but it can be connected to a computer and the sheet music will be made automatically. There are a lot of places you can go on the Net to learn about these systems and hear the music others have created with the technology. Visit any of the sites listed in *MIDI Madness*. Most computers will need special software and maybe even hardware, like a sound card, to run a MIDI system.

MIDI Madness

World Band
http://conect.bbn.com/WorldBand/CoNECTMusic.html

This is a project involving a set of schools whose students are using MIDI synthesizer and computer sequencing software.

Harmony Central
http://harmony-central.mit.edu

The Massachusetts Institute of Technology (MIT) offers a great collection of MIDI tidbits.

The MIDI Home Page
http://www.eeb.ele.tue.nl/midi/index.html

In addition to a long list of additional MIDI sites, you can get an introduction to MIDI here.

Starting a Band

The best way to test your new songs or musical ideas is to get a group of musicians together to play your composition. As you play what you have created, you can make adjustments as you go. Hearing a song inside your head can be very different from the way it sounds when it's played with real instruments. That's the great thing about composing. Until you hear something you like, you just keep trying—and don't forget to have fun in the process! And you don't have to buy expensive

instruments; you make your own from things you find around your house. Ever put beans or rice in a can to create a percussion instrument? Ever used a spoon to tap a bunch of glasses that have different amounts of water?

As you continue to create new pieces, you will become a more experienced composer and may not need to make many adjustments at all. You may want to stay in touch with new happenings in music and what is available through the Internet by subscribing to the sites listed in *Staying Up to Date*. Be on the lookout for new places on the Internet to send a file of your music; these places will gain in popularity with the growth of the World Wide Web, and they will offer a great way to let others hear your music.

Staying Up to Date

New-Releases

Subscribe to majordomo@cs.uwp.edu, a low-volume list that sends one file every week about upcoming album releases.

Music Resources

Join by sending e-mail to rec.music.info. It is a Usenet group with information about music resources on the Internet: FTP sites, music newsgroups, mailing lists, discographies, concert dates, chart listings, and new releases.

All Star Magazine
http://allstarmag.com/news

Musicians of all shapes and sizes are addressed in the pages of *All Star Magazine*.

NOTE

Sound files are just like files of text or graphics, and you can upload them to the Internet in similar ways. Check with your local computer store to find out what sound utilities you need on your home computer so that you can send, receive, and hear music files.

HOT! HOT! HOT!

AMG All-Music Guide
http://allmovie.com/amg/music_root.html

This is a complete online database of recorded music. Just type in an artist, album, or song title and get more information than you thought imaginable!

Musi-Cal
http://concerts.calendar.com

This is a gateway to live music.

Latin Music On-Line!
http://www.lamusica.com

If you like Luis Miguel, you'll love this site!

Chicks Rock
http://www.media.ku.dk/students/anya/CHICKS.htm

This site is dedicated to women rockers and includes interviews, artists, new bands, books, and essays.

Internet Underground Music Archive
http://www.iuma.com

This is a music archive for all kinds of bands and musicians that are relatively unknown.

CyberKids/CyberTeens Young Composers
http://www.cyberkids.com/composers/composers.html

If you really get the composing bug, find some like-minded friends at this site.

The Zine Zone

In the old days (that is, before the Internet), publishers of magazines, newspapers, and books decided whose writing to include in a publication. Since it costs a lot of money to put these publications together and print them, it usually meant that there were too many writers for too few pages of paper. That was then.

This is now! Today people all over the world are becoming their own publishers by posting their own work on the Web. It doesn't cost very much money, and every writer on the Web has potentially huge audience of readers all over the world. Zines are popping up like dandelions these days.

The Publishing Desk

You already have everything it takes to become a published author. You have creativity, motivation, and, by following these steps, directions for submitting your work.

1. Write some new fiction or adapt something you have already written.

Obviously you need to have something to submit to an online journal or zine. You may already have written a story, poem, or play by doing some of the projects in this book such as *Writer's Corner* in Chapter 5. If so, pull it out, read it over, and make any changes you think will make it a stronger piece.

If you haven't tried these projects yet, you will need to develop a written piece of work. It can be any type or style—short story, essay, poetry, or movie review—and can be about anything.

2. Share your story with others before submitting it to an online journal.

Once you have a final version of your written piece, you're ready for the next step: finding someone to publish it. However, before you start submitting your story to different journals and zines, you may want to have a few people read it and give you their impressions and comments.

Student discussion areas exist on the Internet where you can send your manuscript to other aspiring writers. Use the sites in *Online Writing Workshops*, like The Inkspot, shown in Figure 7.4. Asking for direct comments will give you new ideas for how to make your piece stronger and more interesting.

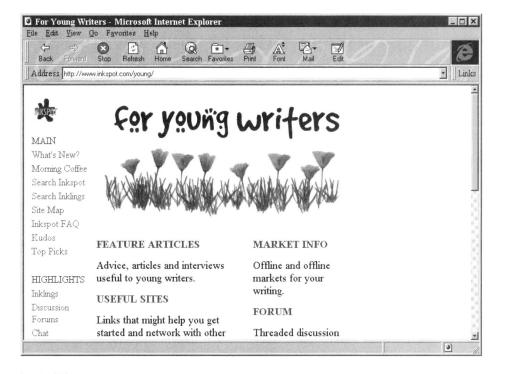

The Inkspot's Resources for Young Writers offers **lots of advice for getting your work published** (http://www.inkspot.com/young).

Online Writing Workshops

The Inkspot for Young Writers
http://www.inkspot.com/young

The Inkspot offers articles, writing contests, and a discussion forum where you can share your writing and get advice from other writers.

The Children and Young Adult Writing Workshop Listserv

subscribe to YAWRITE@LISTS.PSU.EDU

The Young Author's Workshop
http://www.planet.eon.net/~bplaroch/index.html

Learning to give, receive, and use "constructive" feedback—comments that help you improve your writing—are important skills for a writer to have. Use the tips in *Giving Literary Criticism* and *Receiving Literary Criticism* to help you identify those comments that are most helpful and apply them to your work.

Giving Literary Criticism

 Tell the author what you really like about the writing.

 Ask the author what he or she feels are the strengths and weaknesses so you can focus on these points in your comments.

Offer specific suggestions on how the author can make the writing better.

Receiving Literary Criticism

★ Before asking for feedback from others, let them know the aspects of your written work with which you are struggling.

★ Keep in mind that the comments are about your writing, not about you personally.

★ As the author, you should consider all suggestions given to you about your writing; however, only you decide which changes are made.

3. Submit your writing to the appropriate resources.

Now that your story is in final form, send it to as many online publishers listed in *Electronic Literary Journals and Zines* as possible (the home page from *The Vocal Point*, one of these zines, is shown in Figure 7.5). But don't forget the offline magazine, either—you'll always want to keep your eyes open for new places to submit your work. If your story isn't published on the first try, don't be discouraged! You might need to make a few revisions. Be persistent and continue to submit your writing.

Most importantly, though, keep working on your writing. Even Shakespeare had his work rejected!

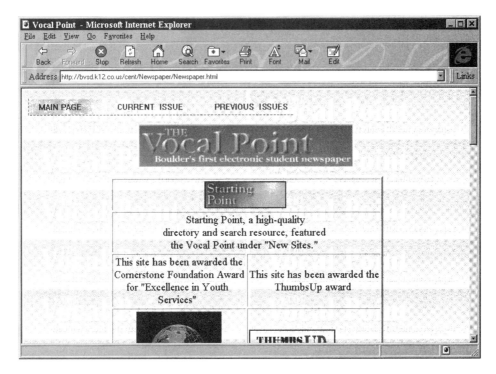

FIGURE 7.5: *The Vocal Point* is designed, managed, and maintained by middle school students (http://bvsd.k12.co.us/cent/Newspaper/Newspaper.html).

Electronic Literary Journals and Zines

The Looking Glass Gazette
http://www.cowboy.net/~mharper/LGG.html

Written and published by kids, this publication focuses on stories, poems, and artwork.

The View from My Window
http://www.youth.net/window/hypermail/index.html

Here students from all over describe what they see out of their windows. It seems like a simple thing to do, but the responses are often beautiful and poetic.

Electronic Literary Journals and Zines (cont.)

The Vocal Point
`http://bvsd.k12.co.us/cent/Newspaper/Newspaper.html`
Written collaboratively by middle school students all over the United States, *The Vocal Point* tackles a new topic in each issue.

Become a regular visitor to several online publications. Often if you subscribe to a printed publication there will be an annual fee. If you want to subscribe to a journal, talk it over with your parents to make sure you can spend your money in this way. As a subscriber, you have the opportunity to read other people's writing and observe different styles and perspectives.

Publish It

Once you become familiar with the world of online publishing, you will know all you need to know about creating your own electronic journal or zine. You will need to collect writing, determine which pieces will be included, create the issue, and distribute it to all who subscribe. You can do all of these tasks with e-mail, the most basic feature of the Internet. The best part about being the publisher is that you get to decide the theme of your zine: essays by teenagers, new poetry, photography, short fiction, and so on. It's up to you!

TIP #7

Your Web zine doesn't have to be a literary journal. It could be a way for you to show off the things you draw, paint, or make out of clay. Your zine could be an online comic book or a biography of your dog. It's up to you, and the sky is the limit!

Creating the Zine

Once you post a message on a listserv or on a Web site asking for people to send you their writing by e-mail, you should have plenty of things to choose from to include in your new zine. Create a word processing file, paste in the pieces you have chosen, and save it as a file in text format. Give your zine a title, and it's ready to be sent to all of your subscribers as an e-mail message. Before you send it out, though, you'll need to ask each author for permission to publish their writing.

In addition to new pieces of writing, you will also receive messages from people wanting to become subscribers to your zine. See Chapter 1 to learn how to create a mailing list to which you can add all of the subscribers' e-mail addresses. Then, once your issue is ready to be sent, you can send it to the list, and the computer will take care of getting it to each individual address.

hello my
fReNch
hOrN sings
to the
cOOL
night...

Better yet, format your zine as you would like, add graphic elements (such as photos, drawings, and navigation symbols), and post a notice about it on a listserv so that everyone who subscribes to that listserv can read your publication (see Chapter 9 for help posting things to the Web).

The Internet makes writing and publishing more accessible and fun than it ever was in the past. Take advantage of this global information network; put your zine out there!

HOT! HOT! HOT!

MidLink Magazine
http://longwood.cs.ucf.edu/~MidLink

This e-zine is written by kids for kids in middle school, and it is an award-winning showcase for young creative writers.

A Vision
http://www.igc.apc.org/iearn/projects/av.html

An I*EARN project, this literary magazine publishes art, poetry, and prose created by secondary school students from all over the world.

Inklings
http://www.inkspot.com/inklings

Besides serving as a resource for young writers (see *Online Writing Workshops*), *The Inkspot* publishes a nifty lit zine, called *Inklings*.

Children's Writings
http://www.ucalgary.ca/~dkbrown/writings.html

This is a fantastic source for really good kids' writing. Use it for inspiration and entertainment or as a place to get yourself published.

Going to the Experts

Going to the experts is a great way get information about questions you have. In almost any area you can imagine, there are people who study and think about that topic. Through the Internet, you can contact these experts directly. The projects in this chapter will help you find the tools you need to go to the source:

★ *Web Weather Watchers* lets you be the expert to help others learn how the weather will impact them tomorrow, next week, and even next year.

★ *Direct Connection to the Experts* includes great ideas for bringing your questions about the world—whether they're about science or sports—to an expert in the field.

★ *Web Watchdog* lets you ask the question, "Should I believe what I see on the Web?" and discover who the experts *really* are.

Web Weather Watchers

Think you can predict the weather? Give it a shot with this project by learning about weather patterns. You will find many resources on the Internet with current data on weather, including temperatures, images of weather events and weather patterns, and predictions from people who observe the weather. With a little practice and *Web Weather Watchers*, you can anticipate what the weather is going to be in the near future—or at least find out over the Internet.

Before the study of weather—called *meteorology*—became a popular science, people used myths to predict and forecast the weather. Most of the myths listed here try to explain natural *phenomena* (events):

★ If there is a ring around the moon, it's going to rain tomorrow.

★ If the sky is orange, a tornado is on the way.

★ If a dog squeals and is restless, a lightning storm will strike soon.

★ You can tell how many miles away a storm is by counting the number of seconds between a stroke of lightning and a boom of thunder.

What other weather sayings do you know?

Now, it's become a true science with many weather monitoring and research stations helping meteorologists develop weather predictions and forecasts for television news, newspapers, radio, and the Internet. Their work and the information they provide is very valuable. It may take many meteorologists hours of research and observation to create an accurate five-minute weather forecast.

Because there are different factors that affect the weather—like wind, rain levels, land formations, volcanoes, and ocean currents—making predictions can be difficult. However, it's important to meet the challenge, because weather conditions have a *profound* (extensive) effect on farming, construction, travel, and our everyday lives.

The Internet feature you will use in this project is the Web.

Becoming an Amateur Meteorologist

Even though it takes many years of training in school to become a meteorologist, you can begin as an amateur weather observer.

1. Choose several locations in the world to monitor.

Weather happens 24 hours a day, everywhere in the world. At any given moment, places have sunshine, rain, snow, freezing temperatures, high winds, or other weather conditions.

Using a world atlas or a map of the United States, choose two or three locations to observe every day for some period of time, such as several days,

Finding a City's Global Address

A city's *latitude* is the distance, measured in degrees, from the equator, the line which separates the Northern and Southern Hemispheres. A city's *longitude* is the distance, measured in degrees, from the *prime meridian*, an imaginary vertical line that runs through Greenwich, England.

For example, the global address for Washington, D.C., is 38 degrees North, 77 degrees West. This is its global address no matter where you are in the world. A location's longitude and latitude is a standard address that will never change.

a week, or even a month. Try to pick locations that are different from each other. You could try comparing Fairbanks, Alaska, or Miami, Florida, to Honolulu, Hawaii. Or you could pick a large city near where you live. Perhaps you'll want to select places 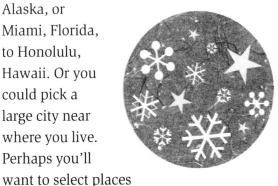 with different climates. Take a look at a city's *altitude* (vertical distance from sea level), as well as its latitude and longitude, to find its "global address." Look at a city's weather on the Web by going to The Weather Channel (`http://www.weather.com`).

You may also want to choose places that are more likely to experience extreme weather situations. For instance, the Caribbean islands prepare for hurricanes during a season that lasts from May through November, while the coast of Thailand prepares for typhoons (heavy rains) from June through September. In the United States, the Midwest is prone to tornadoes from May to August.

Because many of the weather services on the Internet provide information for major cities around the world, it will be helpful to identify large cities with high populations as observation locations.

2. Observe weather conditions on a daily basis.

The Web hosts many sites that provide daily and even hourly updates on weather conditions around the world. Begin by using one of the Web sites listed in *Where to Get Weather Data*.

Where to Get Weather Data

Weather Underground
http://groundhog.sprl.umich.edu

The Weather Channel Online
http://www.weather.com

National Science Foundation's Geoscience Data Server
http://atm.geo.nsf.gov

NASA's K-12 Weather Page
http://www.athena.ivv.nasa.gov/curric/weather/index.html

If your computer has sufficient memory, and your Internet connection is fast enough, you will be able to look at satellite photos of weather from space. These images will give you a good idea of how storms look and move.

Use these Web sites and other weather-related resources (your local news, national weather forecasts on TV's CNN and the Weather Channel) to find data about the locations you are observing. In addition to temperature highs and lows, you may also want to note the barometric pressure (air pressure), wind levels or speed, and amounts of rain (also called *precipitation*). Other facts, such as moon stages, tides, hours of daylight, and seasons, may be interesting to track as well. Figure 8.1 shows a great site you can visit for all kinds of weather maps.

You can keep your notes in a notebook or in a computer spreadsheet. (Check with your parents or teacher to find out whether you have access to spreadsheet software, such as Microsoft's Excel.) The advantage of using a computer spreadsheet, is that it will be easy to create charts to demonstrate changes and make comparisons of weather conditions.

If a storm is occurring, you can track its path using your map or atlas. On a regular basis—perhaps two times a day—stick a pin on your map to indicate the position of the storm. As it moves, your pins will illustrate the storm's path. Save the satellite photos you get from the Web to show the size and shape of the storm.

3. Identify weather patterns.

After you have recorded at least one week's worth of observations, you may be able to identify repetitive patterns in the weather. For instance, is there always a brief rain shower in the mid-afternoon in one of the cities you are observing? Or is there a consistent temperature range right before a thunderstorm? Do the tides affecting a coastal city follow consistent patterns?

If you can keep up your observations for a full month, you can look at other factors that may influence weather conditions. For example, do the stages of the moon (new moon, quarter moon, half moon, three-quarters moon, and full moon) affect the weather?

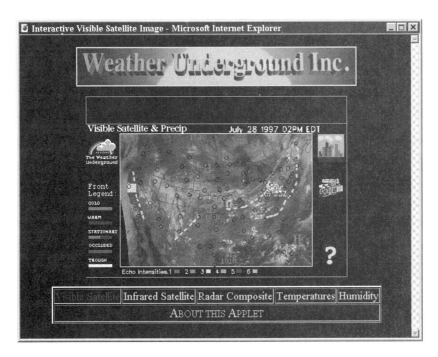

FIGURE 8.1:   **The Weather Underground offers Mac, Windows, and Java versions of an interactive map that allows you to zoom in on certain cities and look for only the data that you want** (http://groundhog .sprl.umich.edu/BS.html)**.**

As you continue to observe changes in weather, ask yourself a few questions:

★ How do mountain ranges affect precipitation levels?

★ How does altitude affect temperatures?

★ Do storms move differently when they are over water or over land?

Several of the resources listed in the Hotlist provide images of weather events that you can download onto your computer.

4. Predict the weather for one location.

After you've identified a few patterns, your observations can help you predict future weather conditions. With one of the locations you have observed, predict what the high and low temperatures may be one day in advance. See if you can predict other aspects of the weather, such as when it will rain or snow.

TIP

Since weather patterns generally move from west to east, you can bet that a storm affecting Pennsylvania today will rain on New York tomorrow. When you look at weather maps online, try to spot these predictable patterns. You will find that your predictions are more accurate!

As your predictions get closer to what really happens, try to extend your forecast for a few days in advance, although even meteorologists have a hard time predicting more than five days ahead. If your predictions are different from what actually happens, you can always try again the next day.

Planning Ahead

How many times has an event that you wanted to attend been canceled because of rain or snow? Perhaps you are on a sports team that plays outdoors. Your ability to predict the weather could be a very valuable skill to your team. You could become a personal weather forecaster for your family and friends. Suggest to people what activities they may want to prepare for as a result of your weather forecast. Here are a few ideas:

★ Sailing is best on a windy day, but not when a storm is predicted.

★ Skiing is best on a cold, but not freezing, day just after fresh snow has fallen.

★ Football and cycling are best on cool, sunny days.

You can also warn your friends about dangerous weather conditions:

★ Don't go skiing today, because the temperatures are too cold and you might get frostbite.

★ Don't go running today because both the humidity and temperature are very high and you could suffer from heat exhaustion.

★ Don't go in the water this afternoon because lightning has been sighted, and lightning is attracted to water.

Weather Prediction Contest

www.webweatherwatchers.com

If you find that several of your friends are also interested in observing weather conditions, create a contest for predicting the weather. Identify one location and tell everyone to make a prediction for the next day's weather. Set a deadline, such as 5:00 P.M. Check the actual weather data the next day and see who has the closest prediction.

Weather can be very unpredictable, so always be on the lookout for unusual conditions. With practice, you will see some interesting patterns and perfect your meteorological skills.

HOT! HOT! HOT!

Blue Skies
http://groundhog.sprl.umich.edu

Check out this special software through the Weather Underground. Called Blue Skies, it allows you to view and manipulate interactive weather maps.

NASA's Ocean Color Seen from Space
http://www.athena.ivv.nasa.gov/curric/oceans/ocolor/index.html

This is NASA's collection of informative satellite photos and other images that illustrate how dynamic and full of life the ocean is, giving you lots of clues to how weather behaves as it crosses the water.

HOT! HOT! HOT!

World Wide Web Tide Predictor
http://tbone.biol.sc.edu/tide/sitesel.html

This online tide calculator is a terrific resource for studying and predicting how the ocean's tides will affect coastal cities all over the world.

Institute of Global Environment and Society Weather Page
http://grads.iges.org/pix/wxmaps.html

Here you can get maps, forecasts, data (updated every hour), and three-day predictions.

***USA Today* Weather**
http://usatoday.com/weather/wfront.htm

Everything you need to know about today's weather in the United States can be found here. You can also send a specific question to the weather editor of the paper and Web site.

Dan's Wild Wild Weather Page
http://www.whnt19.com/kidwx/index.htm

This site includes a link to a forecasting computer.

Dan Satterfield is the weather guy for WHNT-TV, Channel 19, in Huntsville, Alabama. He brings together great information about all kinds of weather patterns and events.

Direct Connection to the Experts

NOTE

Although the Net provides an amazing amount of resources to help you find answers to questions you have, sometimes you just need to talk to an expert. An expert: the wise one who knows how to make a perfect swing of a club or how to work out a complex and difficult mathematical formula. The Net can help you connect directly to these experts so that you can benefit from their extensive knowledge and experience.

Wouldn't it be cool to have a phone that goes right to the President? Or how about to the number one tennis player in the world? Anytime you had a question you could just pick up the phone, make a call, and get an answer from an expert.

Unfortunately, a phone like this doesn't exist. However, you can use the Net to find experts and send them your questions via e-mail. They can help you with your homework, your golf game, movie reviews, or just random questions in general. No question is too strange to be asked. In fact, maybe you'll end up stumping an expert!

I need an expert!

Eight: Going to the Experts

 The Internet features you will use in this project are e-mail and the Web.

Your Quest for the Wise One

1. What's your question?

Think about things that spark your curiosity. If you are stumped for a good question, just look around you in nature (or take a shot at your homework!)—there are questions everywhere! Once you have written out your question, you will use the Internet to send it in an e-mail message to an expert. After giving the expert enough time to research and answer your question, you can check your e-mail for a response. It's that easy!

Ever wondered about these things:

⭐ What is a rainbow?

⭐ Who has thrown the most touchdown passes in the NFL?

⭐ How do you build a treehouse?

⭐ How many galaxies exist in the universe?

2. Present your question to the wise one.

If you have a question about science, you are in luck! There are many sites on the Net that give you access to all kinds of scientists—from astronomers to volcanologists. If you visit Yahooligans!, and go into the homework area, you will find a long list of sites that connect you to these different scientists. (Look at the list in Figure 8.2). You can also visit the sites listed in *Ask a Scientist*. You might even try posting a question in several different places and then compare the answers you receive.

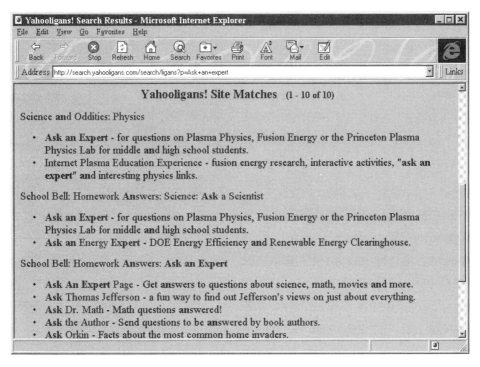

FIGURE 8.2: **Yahooligans! has a great list of sites that connect you and your question to the right kind of scientist.**

Ask a Scientist

NASA Spacelink
http://spacelink.nasa.gov

For every shuttle mission, there is a way for you to send e-mail messages to the astronauts in space.

Ask Dr. Math
http://forum.swarthmore.edu/dr.math/dr-math.html

Whether you are in elementary, middle, high school, or even college you can send your math question to Dr. Math and get help with it. Check the archives first and then send your question to the doctor (see Figure 8.3).

Ask a Scientist or Engineer
http://www.nsf.gov/od/lpa/nstw/quests/start.htm

A project of the National Science Foundation, this site puts you in touch with real scientists and engineers who can lend their wealth of experience to your questions about the world.

Ask a High-Energy Astronomer
http://asca.gsfc.nasa.gov/docs/learning_center/ask_astro/ask_an_astronomer.html

Have questions about X-rays or gamma ray astronomy? Go here!

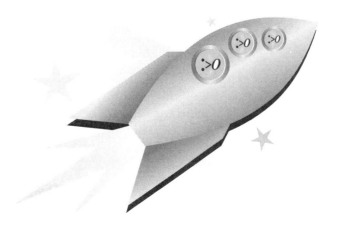

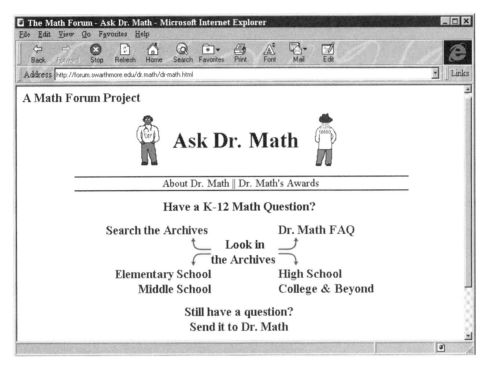

A Math Forum Project

Ask Dr. Math

About Dr. Math ‖ Dr. Math's Awards

Have a K-12 Math Question?

Search the Archives   Dr. Math FAQ

Look in
the Archives

Elementary School   High School
Middle School   College & Beyond

Still have a question?
Send it to Dr. Math

FIGURE 8.3: **Whether you are 5 or 55, Dr. Math can help you solve the mathematical problems you face!**

If your question is outside the scientific arena, your options are a bit more limited but not completely absent. More and more organizations are putting together "ask an expert" programs. Explore the sites in *Expert Connections* as well as at the Hotlist at the end of this project. As you can see from Figure 8.4, there are many different categories of experts.

Expert Connections

Ask an Expert
http://www.askanexpert.com/askanexpert

This site advertises "Free advice from the Amish to zoo keeping!" You can select from 12 categories with more than 300 Web sites and e-mail addresses where you can find experts to answer your questions.

Ask the Author
http://www.ipl.org/youth/AskAuthor/AskAuthor.html

The Internet Public Library has enlisted a group of youth authors and illustrators to answer your questions about literature.

Cool Kids with Clubs
http://www.pga.com/2

Want to swing a club like Tiger Woods? Contact Steve Jubb, golf pro expert.

3. Be patient for an answer.

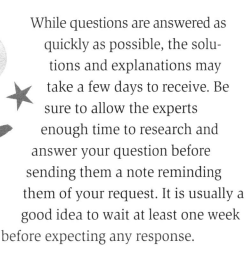

While questions are answered as quickly as possible, the solutions and explanations may take a few days to receive. Be sure to allow the experts enough time to research and answer your question before sending them a note reminding them of your request. It is usually a good idea to wait at least one week before expecting any response.

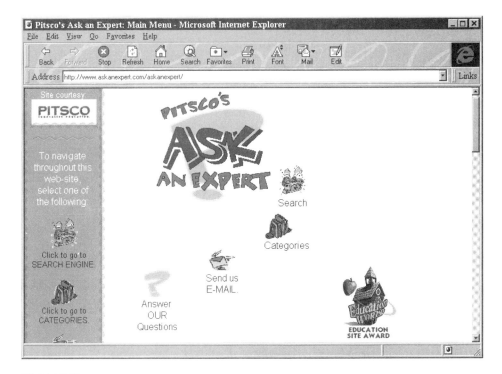

FIGURE 8.4: **Sponsored by a company and staffed by a number of volunteer experts, the Ask an Expert page (`http://www.askanexpert.com/ askanexpert`) can link you to the best.**

Remember, if you send your question on a Friday night, the expert might not look at it until the next week.

You Be the Expert

What do you think you know more than anyone else in the world? What do spend a lot of your time on? Maybe you are an expert and help answer other people's questions!

Maybe you do find science interesting. Look around your community. Is your drinking water being tested for toxic chemicals? What is the recycling plan? How much acid is in your rainfall? If you tackle local problems with scientific research, the people who make the decisions will take you seriously and may listen to your concerns.

Start a Club

With some friends, start a scientific explorers club. Brainstorm to come up with tough questions. Have each person think of a question on a different topic to post online and then use the answers to learn with each other about different types of science.

HOT! HOT! HOT!

New Jersey's Ask An Expert Page
http://njnie.dl.stevens-tech.edu/curriculum/aska.html

Although this site is supported by New Jersey businesses, anyone on the Internet can use the service that categorizes experts by categories.

Ask Ken!
http://www.efn.org/~andrec/ask_ken.html

You may not know who Ken is, but he is the "Dear Abby" of the Web.

HOT! HOT! HOT!

Kids Did This!
http://sln.fi.edu/tfi/hotlists/kids.html

The Franklin Institute Science Museum maintains this collection of links to projects in all kinds of subject areas done by kids and teens. Find ideas for school projects of your own or just see what other people are doing.

The Yuckiest Site on the Internet
http://www.nj.com/yucky

Explore all of the gross things in the world and have a good time doing it.

Web Watchdog

This project will show you how to analyze and get the most out of sites you visit on the Web. As a *Web Watchdog*, you will use different strategies to examine what issues are being presented and how they are presented. You will know what questions to ask yourself any-time you look at a new site. You'll be a smarter Netizen.

You can be a watchdog—not the kind that sits in front of a dark house at night, but the kind that surveys the Web to report on how information is presented.

sniffing out the truth

As a watchdog, you will no longer be a passive consumer of information; you'll have lots of questions to ask when you explore the Web. In finding answers to your questions and evaluating what you read, see, and hear, you will develop important thinking skills and also make your use of the Web more productive.

Watchdogs also help people do their jobs better. As a watchdog, you can inform the person or organization behind each Web site about problems or mistakes in their sites. Most Web sites have a Contact link or e-mail address so that you can be a Web watchdog. Sybex, the publisher of this book, has their own feedback section on their Web site (see Figure 8.5).

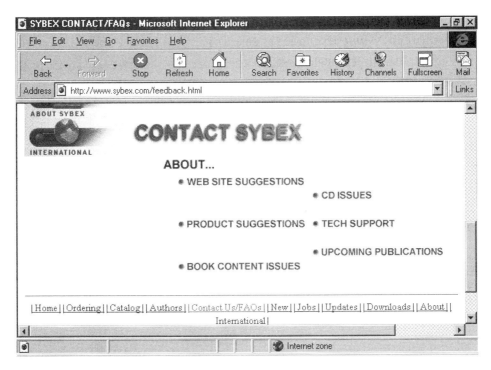

FIGURE 8.5: **You can send your comments to Sybex at** `http://www.sybex.com/feedback.html`.

NOTE

The Internet features you will use for this project
are e-mail and the Web.

Surveying the Scene

Just as surveyors examine a piece of land for future construction, you can survey the Web to see what is there.

1. Choose an area of the Web to survey.

To begin your survey of the Web, you should limit the amount of information you are tracking so you can really concentrate and draw conclusions. You might decide that you want to compare sites devoted to a certain cause or issue or public person. Examples would be endangered species, race relations, and President Bill Clinton.

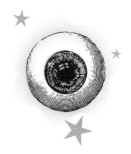

2. Identify the sources you will use.

Choosing too many Web sites to survey can be overwhelming, so limit the number to less than 10. You will therefore be able to go into greater depth at each site.

Search engines and indices will be of help in finding sites related to your topic. Online news organizations are also rich in information on more recent events, organizations, and people. Comparing them can be very illuminating, too, since each organization handles the news differently. See *News on the Net* for some of these news outlets.

News on the Net

The Washington Post Online
http://www.washingtonpost.com

The New York Times
http://www.nytimes.com

Cable News Network (CNN)
http://www.cnn.com

MSNBC
http://www.msnbc.com

ABC News
http://www.abcnews.com

3. Choose one research perspective.

A research perspective can usually be expressed in the form of a question. Here are some examples for examining news sites and the articles they contain regarding the coverage of the president's actions:

★ What is the length of all stories that contain information about the president? Does one newspaper have longer articles than another?

★ Where are articles that contain information about the president positioned? On the front page? Third page of the business section?

★ What is the frequency of coverage, or how many articles are there that contain information about the president?

Once you have decided on the research perspective you want to take, try to write your own questions. Make the questions as clear as you can.

4. Monitor the coverage.

★ Now you are just about ready to begin your research by monitoring the coverage of an issue in several newspapers. The only decision you still need to make is when you are going to end the monitoring. Decide how much time you can spend on monitoring every day. Be realistic. Perhaps you'll spend an hour a day for one week, one month, or even a year (if you are a *really* ambitious watchdog).

WATCH IT

5. Report your findings.

As with all research, it is important to report your findings to other people in the community who are interested in what the media are doing and how they are covering current issues. Share your observations with family, friends, and others on the Internet. You may even be able to submit it as a school project. Write a one-page description of your conclusions. Here are a few questions you may want to ask yourself

before you write about what you found con-
cerning coverage of the president's actions:

⭐ Were articles about the president always
longer on one of the Web sites?

⭐ Were articles about the
president always on the
front page regardless of
other important events?

⭐ Was there an article about
the president every day on
one site and only once a week
on another?

As you look at your monitoring sheet, what conclusions can you
make? In addition to your written description, you should be able to
create a few graphs to demonstrate large differences. For example, a
graph can show how many times each ran an article about the president,
or whatever your topic is.

Write back! When you have visited a site several times, you will probably have some ideas
for the people who put it up. Don't be shy
about contacting the author or the Webmaster
who maintains the site with your ideas. And if
you notice an error in the site, they will be
glad that you told them about it so that they can
then fix it.

Evaluating Web Sites

When you go to any Web site, there are some questions that you will probably want to answer for yourself. If you answer *yes* to all of these questions, the site is probably very good. Try these out on the next site you visit!

★ Is the information accurate?

★ Is the information delivered by a reliable source?

★ Is the information objective and unbiased (not leaning toward a certain opinion or perspective)?

★ Does the site contain enough information to cover the subject?

★ Is the site updated and maintained regularly?

★ Is there some way to get in touch with the author or Webmaster?

★ If the site has advertisements on it, are they small and out of the way?

★ Is the information well organized and clear?

Don't forget: Never give out your home street address or phone number over the Web without a parent's permission.

Exploring the Watchdog Frontiers

You can be a watchdog of many types of media: not just newspapers, but also television news shows, magazines, movies made for television—you name it. If people know that you and others are out there checking on what they are doing in the media, they might think more carefully about what they write.

Create a Media Watchdog Team

Because there are newspapers in almost every city or town, you can enlist a whole team of watchdogs to survey the same issue across numerous sources. This is an excellent way to expand the reach of your surveying. People from different states and even different countries can explore how media coverage changes by region and country. Recruit your team and exchange what you find through e-mail and a Web site!

HOT! HOT! HOT!

Internet Safety
http://www.uoknor.edu/oupd/kidsafe/inet.htm

Everything you need to know to be "Web safe."

Magellan Internet Services
http://www.mckinley.com

This searchable index of Internet links will allow you to limit your searches to only the kid-friendly "Green Light" sites.

Internet Tutorial
http://www.msn.com/tutorial/default.html

This "Netiquette" resource from Microsoft will teach you lots about the Internet and how to use it.

Understanding and Using the Internet
http://www.pbs.org/uti

This site, put up by PBS (Public Television), will give you some background on this crazy computer network.

<HTML>

my vacation in
RIO DE JANEIRO

WHAT'S
HOT?
¿NOT
the pulse
OF OUR
GENERATION

<BUILDING COOL SITES>

ET FVGIT INTEREA FVGIT
IRREPARABILE TEMPVS

WELCOME
to my world

aRT

aBoUt mE

fUn sTuFf

HI, YALL!
welcome
TO
Tuscumbia,
ALABAMA
✳✳✳✳
PROUD BIRTHPLACE
OF
HELLEN
KELLER

<BODY>
<B>Welcome to my world</B>
<BODY>
</HTML>

Building Cool Sites on the Web

Surfing the Web is fun, but why just browse when you can build? That's right—you, too, can stake out your claim to a parcel of the information frontier. And it's easier than you think!

What sets the Internet apart from media like TV and books and newspapers is its ability to support two-way communication. In other words, you can talk back to this medium—and it will hear you! Imagine if you could add your own thoughts to a news broadcast you were watching on TV. Now imagine that you could broadcast your own news show. That is what the World Wide Web is all about: talking and listening, sending and receiving.

★ *Building My Page on the Net* gives you the tools you need to build a home page on the Web that the whole world can see.

★ *My Piece of the Planet* will show you how to think globally by researching locally.

★ *My Generation* will spur you to activism as you search for answers to the questions that most concern you about the world.

★ *My Excellent Adventure* is your ticket to publish your travel journals online!

In each of these projects you can build your own piece of the Internet. How you build it is up to you: Like baking a cake, you can make it from scratch or use a ready-made mix in a box. The "from scratch" recipe for Web building is called HTML, or Hypertext Markup Language, a simple programming language.

To see how HTML works when you write it from scratch, try this experiment. Using Notepad or your word processing application, type the following (replacing "*Your Name*" with your first and last name):

```
<HTML>
<HEAD>
<TITLE>My First Web Page</TITLE>
</HEAD>
<BODY BGCOLOR="GOLD" TEXT="BLACK">
<H1>Your Name's First Web Page</H1>
<BODY>
<B>Hello!</B> This is my first Web page!
</BODY>
</HTML>
```

Once you have typed the lines of HTML, save the document as "plain text" (or "text only") and then name it `test.html` (or anything you want with `.html` at the end). Saving the file with `.html` extension is important because that is how a browser will know it is an HTML file. Make a note of where the file is saved on your hard drive (you'll have to find it shortly). Once you have saved the file, open up your Web browser, and go to the File menu and select Open or Open File. Select the document that you have just made (`test.html`) by navigating to where you saved it. (You can choose the Browse option in your browser to find the file.) Once you find the file, click OK to see what it looks like. It should look similar to Figure 9.1.

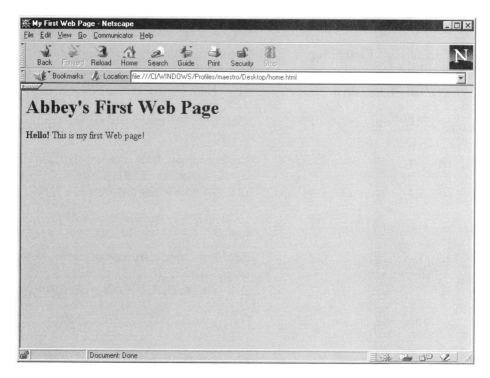

FIGURE 9.1: **You have created your very own page with HTML.**

If you don't see this page, make sure you've typed all the HTML lines correctly, and that you've selected the correct file to display in your Web browser. The lines of HTML that you typed include HTML *tags*. Tags are a way to tell browsers how to display the text contained within the tags. For instance, the line, <TITLE>My First Web Page</TITLE> told your browser to display the text "My First Web Page" as the title of your document. To learn more, see *HTML Tags*.

HTML Tags

Here are some of the tags that you will see when you look at the HTML behind any Web page (most browsers let you "view the source"). The function of each one is listed at the right. Note that most tags (like <HTML>) have an "end" tag (</HTML>) that has a forward slash and ends the function.

<HTML>	</HTML>	Contains the entire HTML document
<TITLE>	</TITLE>	The words between these tags appear in the title bar of your browser
<BODY>	</BODY>	Contains the body of the page
<BODY BGCOLOR="GOLD" TEXT="BLACK">		Makes the background color gold and the text on the page black. Many other colors are available, including BLUE, PINK, PURPLE, YELLOW, and RED.
<B>	</B>	Makes text bold
<I>	</I>	Makes text italic
<P>		new paragraph (the </P> end tag is not required)
<CENTER>	</CENTER>	Puts text and images in the center of the page
<IMG SRC="image.gif">		Inserts the image named image.gif
<A HREF=http://www .amazon.com>		Indicates a link to http://www.amazon.com

To learn more about HTML, check out the sites in *HTML Basics*. The "boxed recipes" do a lot of the programming work for you.

HTML Basics

A lot of places on the Internet can teach you the basics of HTML programming.

A Beginner's Guide to HTML
http://www.ncsa.uiuc.edu/General/Internet/WWW/
HTMLPrimer.html

HTML Land
http://cygnus.campbellsvil.edu/~chgibbs/html.html

HTML Writer
http://www.public.asu.edu/~bot/tger

Create Your Own
http://www.smplanet.com/webpage/webpage.html

You can also use the software found in *Web Building Tools* to help you create your Web pages. Or you can go to TUCOWS at http://www .tucows.com for a choice of several editors.

Web Building Tools

The applications listed below are called HTML *editors*, and they can help you create Web pages without ever writing a single line of HTML. Many companies offer downloadable versions of their products online, so visit their sites to find out.

HyperStudio
(http://www.hyperstudio.com)

Claris Home Page
(http://www.claris.com)

Web Building Tools (cont.)

★ **Microsoft FrontPage & Word 97**
(http://www.microsoft.com/products)

★ **PageMill**
(http://www.adobe.com/prodindex/pagemill/main.html)

★ **Internet Explorer 4.0**
(http://www.microsoft.com/ie)
and Netscape Communicator 4.0
(http://www.netscape.com)
both offer Web authoring tools as well.

This chapter will give you some ideas for creating Web projects of your own. Ultimately, however, it is up to you to decide what you want to share with the world. Whatever your site, though, it's important that you're participating and talking back to the Web!

Building My Page on the Net

NOTE

It seems like almost everybody has a home page on the World Wide Web, a place to describe their hobbies and link to a few other sites. Yawn! Anybody can post a photo of a pet, so why not do something extraordinary? Make your home page more than a home; make it your channel to express yourself to the world.

Your home page is an opportunity to really communicate something to the world about yourself. Do you draw, paint, write poetry, or play the tuba? Well, the season premiere on your Web page should showcase what you do and what you like to say. Go for it!

The Internet features you will use in this project are the Web and HTML authoring tools.

Talk Back on the Web!

You need to do four main things to add your page to the Net. Begin by deciding what to say, finish by actually saying it.

1. Decide what to say and how to say it.

Think about the many ways that you express yourself. Maybe you draw, paint, sing, or even play a musical instrument. Maybe you write stories, poetry, opinion pieces, an autobiography, or factual reports on everything from historical events to current issues that matter to you.

FUN FACTS ABOUT ME:

- brown belt in Karate
- two cats, Buster & Oskar
- can eat six hot dogs in six minutes

You can express yourself in lots of different ways on your home page—you can use everything from pictures to sound! Look at the things you create; think about using your writing, your photographs, your art, or even your expertise on a particular topic to express yourself on your Web page. A great idea is to mix several different media—for example, you can include poems you've written with drawings and a recording of you reading the poems. Be creative!

TIP

You may need to get help to put video and sound into the right format for the Web. If you have any questions, you can ask an adult who is familiar with computers or you can talk to a support person at your Internet service provider.

You have the skills to express yourself and make yourself understood on the Web.

2. Design your page.

Once you've decided what you want to say, outline just how you will accomplish your project. Using plain paper and pencil, sketch the things you want to include and where you will put them on the page. For instance, you might put the title at the top, with a photo or self-portrait smack in the middle of the page. If you are looking for ideas, take a look at what other kids are doing, beginning with Figures 9.2 and 9.3.

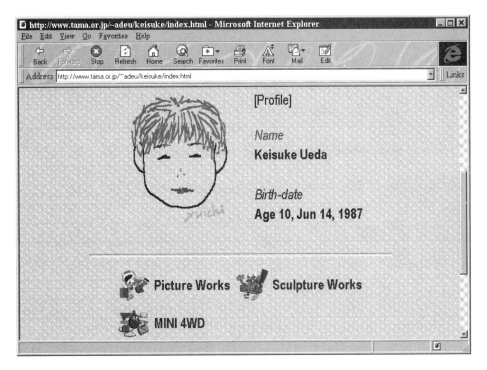

FIGURE 9.2: **You can get great ideas for your home page by looking at other kids' pages. This is where Keisuke, a Japanese girl, shows her art to the world (**`http://www.tama.or.jp/~adeu/keisuke/index.html`**).**

3. Build your Web site.

Building a Web site is not easy, but knowing how to get started will save you lots of time and energy. The first thing you will probably do is to create a basic page format in a Web authoring application; you will make the most basic decisions about how your page will look, from its background color to its use of pictures.

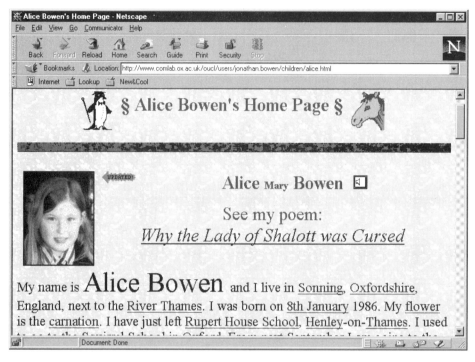

FIGURE 9.3: **Sound files can add a nice, personal touch to a site. Take a look and a listen to this one from an English girl named Alice** (`http://www.comlab.ox.ac.uk/oucl/users/jonathan.bowen/children/alice.html`).

TIP

The best color combinations to use on your Web site are ones that contrast with each other. For example, using light-colored text on a dark background (or the other way around) is a great way to make your site visually distinctive and easy to read. You can also find images and background patterns on the Web (try The Background Boutique at `http://www.geocities.com/SoHo/Lofts/4328`).

Remember: Your site is an ongoing project, so if it doesn't look perfect right away, don't worry. You can (and should) update your site as often as you can.

Since this Web page is about you, keep in mind that some people who come to your site will not know you already, so be clear and make visitors feel welcome. One thing you should avoid, however, is posting your home address or home phone number so that you keep yourself safe from unwanted visitors.

Take a look at some of the thousands of personal home pages out there on the Web by visiting the sites listed in *How to Find Kids' Pages on the Net*. What do you like about them, and what do you dislike? Learn from others' successes and mistakes—it's called innovation!

When you have revised and proofread your site, post your work on a Web server. To do this, you will need space

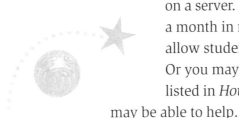

on a server. Internet providers often charge $5—10 a month in rent for this space, and schools often allow students to use space on their own servers. Or you may want to contact some of the groups listed in *How to Find Kids' Pages on the Net* who may be able to help.

Once you have server space, you'll send your Web site files to the server (using FTP, or "file transfer protocol") where they will instantly become public on the Web.

How to Find Kids' Pages on the Net

Yahooligans! has a list of kids' pages inside the categories called "Around the World" and "People" at http://www.yahooligans.com.

GeoCities Enchanted Forest can be found at http://www.geocities.com/EnchantedForest/.

KidLinks connects pages from kids under the age of 13. Go to http://www.geocities.com/CapitolHill/3261/kidlinks.html.

4.   Promote your Web site.

Make the address for your personal Web site a regular part of your e-mail signature (see Chapter 1 for help on doing this). Also, tell your friends to stop watching television and tune into your Web page!

HOT! HOT! HOT!

Hot Dog Express
http://www.sausage.com.au/express.htm

This is a great place to go to build your first Web page. The computer will ask you to answer specific questions and then automatically build a basic page for you. They even provide a place where you can keep your page.

MaMaMedia
http://mamamedia.com/

In addition to games and other neat things for kids, this site allows you to create your own page using sound and pictures they provide.

KidPub
http://www.kidpub.org

This site is dedicated to helping kids publish anything they want on the Web. There are examples, tools, graphics, and fun stuff to help you along the way.

Adam Jones for President in 2024
http://www.mich.com/~jones/

Take the lead from this guy and promote yourself into the future. Adam is serious about his goal and is using the Web to attain it.

My Piece of the Planet

While the Internet is like a global village, it is important to remember that each of us lives in one particular place. Your city or town is unique and special. Now, using the Web and *My Piece of the Planet*, you can share important information about where you live with people all around the world.

Where do you live? In a large city or a small town? Do you live near mountains or the ocean or where it is flat? Did things happen long ago near where you live that didn't happen anywhere else? Are there animals and plants that live and grow in your area that interest you? The answers to all of these questions are good starting points for describing your patch of the planet.

The Internet features you will use in this project are e-mail, the Web, and HTML authoring tools.

What's in Your Backyard?

1. Think about what is most important or interesting about the place that you live.

You might not have thought about it this way before, but the area where you live is unlike any other. It is unique, just like you are! And before you can tell the world about your piece of the planet on the Web, you'll have to think about what you want to say.

HI, YALL!
welcome
TO
Tuscumbia,
ALABAMA
❄ ❄ ❄
PROUD BIRTHPLACE
OF
HELLEN
KELLER

Focus on one thing that is really cool or unusual about your patch of the planet. Your home might be near the site of a Civil War battle, or it might be overrun by grizzly bears every fall. It might be a busy shipping port or a leading producer of mangoes, a hotbed of controversy over forest logging, or home to the world's largest ball of string. Or, your patch of the planet might be interesting for other reasons, like its government, politics, or cultural and educational institutions. But this project is not a tourist brochure; this is about what you think is most important. It's your patch of your world, so you decide.

> Perhaps your city or town already has a Web site. You can start your search for it by using a search engine (see Chapter 1 for advice on how to use search engines). Many community Web sites are established by local libraries and governments, while others are put up by businesses. Two examples are Charlottesville, Virginia's non-profit Monticello Avenue (http://monticello.avenue.gen.va.us) and the commercial CitySearch sites (http://www.citysearch.com).

2. Use your "private-eye" skills.

You'll be surprised how much you can learn by simply asking questions. Ask anyone you can find, including your parents, teachers, librarians, friends, and others. You should be able to reach many knowledgeable people—both locally and elsewhere—through e-mail. Check for e-mail addresses on Web pages that are helpful to your research—whether it is the home page of your local historical society or an international group, you should be able to get in touch with lots of experts by finding e-mail addresses on Web sites.

And since your piece of the planet is all around you, you should be able to learn a lot by simply taking a walk or riding your bike.

If, for example, you are researching the birthplace of a famous person who lived long ago near where you live, make a visit to the birthplace, take pictures, and ask lots of questions. You can also visit your local historical society and public library, and search the Internet for any other information you might be able to find. For past copies of your local newspaper, try the library or the newspaper itself—they'll be glad to help! Soon you'll be an expert, ready to share what you've learned with the world.

As you gather information on your topic, try to stay organized! A good way to keep track of all the cool stuff you'll learn is to take notes, either on note cards or on your computer. Make sure you write down where, from whom, and when you got the information.

3. Design and build your Web site about your patch of the planet.

Now it's time to tell the world what you've learned about your piece of the planet (see Figure 9.4). Ask yourself what would be the most logical way to explain what you want to say, and then write an outline of your major points, starting with an introduction and ending with a conclusion.

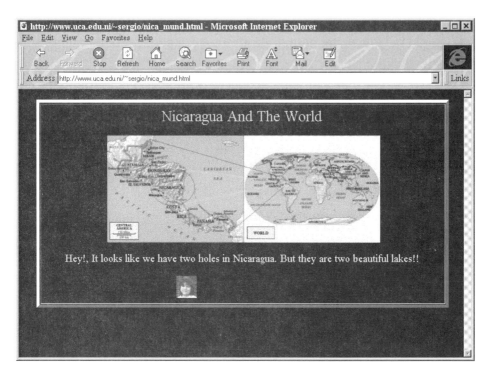

FIGURE 9.4: **Camila from Nicaragua uses a map to show the world her piece of the planet**
(http://www.uca.edu.ni/~sergio/camila.html)**.**

When you are creating your Web site, try to keep pages relatively short (so you don't have to scroll through huge chunks of stuff), use contrasting colors, and add pictures and illustrations to make it interesting for your visitors to look at!

When you have revised and proofread your Web site, post your work on a Web server. Ask your school's technology coordinator or a technician from your Internet service provider for help.

4. Promote your piece of the planet.

With all the hard work you have put into your project, you wouldn't want it just to *sit* there, would you? Tell people about it!

Contact the Webmasters of related Web sites and ask them to provide links to your site (You can usually find the Webmaster's e-mail address at the bottom of a Web page). You can return the favor by linking to their site from yours. This will help to publicize both sites and provide additional materials and context to your visitors. E-mail your friends and classmates, and announce the publication of your site on relevant listservs. Also, you can add your site's URL to the "signature" file in your e-mail program to remind everyone where your piece of the planet is.

HOT! HOT! HOT!

Our Town
http://www.tcfn.org/ourtown.htm

With the motto, "Everyone can do it," the Computer Learning Foundation has started this initiative to get communities, individuals, and schools to make their presence felt on the Web.

The Blacksburg, Virginia Electronic Village
http://www.bev.net

This Virginia town is wired! The entire population of this small town is online, and at their site you can learn just about anything you would want to know about Blacksburg, from the distant past and up to the present.

HOT! HOT! HOT!

USA CityLink
`http://www.usacitylink.com/visitcity.html`

This site offers the Web's most comprehensive listing of U.S. states and cities that provide information on the Web. Choose a city and check it out—it'll give you lots of ideas for creating your own Web page!

My Generation

Got questions about the world around you? Think no one understands your generation? The Internet is a great place to ask questions and to learn more about what's happening all over the planet. Ask questions and gather opinions, then take all the answers you get, put them on the Web and make people listen to your generation!

When you ask lots of people the same questions, you are taking a *poll* (or survey). During elections, newspapers and TV news shows will take opinion polls to find out how voters are thinking. Another kind of poll may be found in your city's newspaper or magazine where people vote for their favorite restaurants and stores.

This project involves working with other kids to take a poll and then study the responses that you have received. At the end, you will be able to chart and publish your results on the Web!

The Internet features you will use in this project are e-mail, the Web, and HTML authoring tools.

What in the World Is Going On?

There is so much happening in the world but how can you *really* know how people think about different issues? Take a poll!

1. Recruit your polling team.

No one person can poll enough people to come up with significant findings. Therefore, you will need to enlist the help of other kids to develop a team of pollsters. And since kids who live close to you will probably receive similar responses to yours, try to enlist the help of kids who live in other parts of the country or the world. One

way to do that would be to post a notice about your poll on your Web page. Another would be to announce what you are trying to do on a relevant listserv. Or you can conduct your poll all by yourself if you prefer.

2. Determine what you want to find out and how you want to ask it.

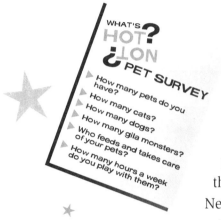

WHAT'S HOT? ¿LON PET SURVEY
- How many pets do you have?
- How many cats?
- How many dogs?
- How many gila monsters?
- Who feeds and takes care of your pets?
- How many hours a week do you play with them?

If you could get inside other people's heads, what would you be looking for? What is the most interesting or troubling question you have for the world today? Think about it and then come up with the big question you want to answer. For example, "What attitudes do people hold about computer technology in this country and elsewhere in the world?"

Next, brainstorm a list of questions related to the central question For example: "Do you enjoy using the Internet?"; "Do you use a computer for work?"; "Do you use a computer to play games?"; and "How many hours per day do you use a computer?" These will help you answer your big, central question. See *Sample Poll of Kids' Musical Interests* for one example.

Sample Poll of Kids' Musical Interests

Big question: *Do you like listening to music?*
Yes   No

How many CDs do you buy a month?
None   1-2   3-5   5-10   More than 10

How many hours a day do you listen to music?
None   1-3   3-5   More than 5

What is your favorite type of music?
Rap   Grunge   Country   Blues   Jazz   Alternative

Do you read music magazines?
Yes   No

Do you watch MTV?
Yes   No

Involve the entire group of pollsters you have assembled in the process of creating good and interesting questions. See *Polling Ideas* if you need help getting started.

Polling Ideas

Stuck for a good question to ask? Well, just think about the world around you—for almost everything that happens or doesn't happen, somebody has an opinion. Consider politics, wars, sports, social issues, and culture. Still nothing comes to mind? Here are some hints:

★ **How do young people feel about the environment?**

★ **Do young people respond to advertising?**

★ **What values are most important to my generation?**

★ **What can we do to change the world?**

How you ask your questions will affect how they are answered. Avoid bias whenever possible—in other words, keep your own opinions to yourself. Also, it is best to ask only questions that can be answered with yes, no, or a number. This makes it easier to compare the answers at the end.

Check out Figure 9.5 to see a poll in action.

3. Ask your questions.

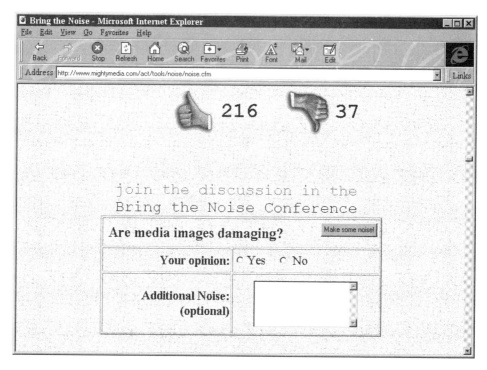

FIGURE 9.5: **The Youth in Action site includes a poll with a question that changes every month** (`http://www.mightymedia.com/act/tools/noise/noise.cfm`).

You can ask your list of questions in one of two ways. First, you may want to ask only a certain group of people—say, kids between the ages of 8 and 10—or perhaps only people from a certain geographical area. In this case, you will probably be able to conduct your survey at school or in your neighborhood.

Another way to conduct your poll is to ask people to fill out a form on the Web. This way, people from all over the world can answer the questions. You might also consider taking surveys on a regular basis with different questions each time. Keep your questionnaires short so that many people will be able to take the time to fill them out.

4. Tell the world what you found.

When you receive the responses to your questions, add up the numbers of like responses to each question and chart them in a report that explains your conclusions and any unexpected results you might have gotten. Then put your results up on the Web so that the rest of the team (and the rest of the world) can be more in touch with your generation.

TIP

If you need help designing your polling page, use the Web publishing tools listed at the beginning of this chapter to create your own Web page. You can also send e-mail to other kids that have created their own Web pages.

HOT! HOT! HOT!

KidStation
http://www.ingenius.com/kids/poll.htm

This site takes the pulse of kids today by posing a new question each week about different issues. They also provide a link to the results of their previous polls.

Too Cool for Grownups
http://www.tcfg.com/interactive.html

Six times a year you can enter your votes for "What's Hot" and "What's Not" on issues that range from food to movies to TV shows.

Cyberatlas
http://www.cyberatlas.com

Go to this site to see an example of how to compile a great deal of information. Cyberatlas tracks statistics on the use of the Internet.

My Excellent Adventure

You have lots of opportunities to join a virtual expedition on the Web. You can use your browser to visit Web sites that show you what it looks like on the surface of Mars. Or you can get daily updates from climbers on Mount Everest and bicyclists in the jungles of Belize.

NOTE

The Internet offers everyone the opportunity to become a virtual wayfarer, a world traveler who never leaves home. But it doesn't have to be that way—why not invite the virtual world along when you really hit the road? Record what happens when you go on a trip and then invite your Web pals to see what you did on the Web.

And while you might not bike through the jungle or climb Himalayan mountains, you do occasionally travel. And when you go places, you are doing some of the same things that these scientists, explorers, and adventurers are doing. This is your chance to bring the world along with you, to see what you see as you travel (or after you travel)—whether it's a

trip to a national park, Disneyland, or to your grandmother's house. It could even be a school field trip!

The Internet features you will use in this project are e-mail, the Web, and HTML authoring tools.

Where Do You Go?

Take the world along on your next trip. Be the eyes and ears for other people on your excellent adventure. Check out *Virtual Excursions* in Chapter 6 for ideas of how to be another person's eyes and ears.

1. On your next trip (of any kind), collect as much information as you can.

Even before you leave home, you can learn about what you will see. Check with your library, ask your parents, and surf the Web for clues to what your trip will be like. Once you're on the plane, the train, or in the

car, keep your eyes and ears open. Keep a journal of what's going on around you and what you see so you won't forget anything, and take pictures if you have access to a camera. You can even record sounds with a tape recorder.

As always, ask lots of questions. Try to learn a variety of things about the places you visit on your journey: You might even find out that seemingly different things like geology, climate, and economics are related and help make that place unique.

2. When you return from your journey, tell the story.

When writing any sort of composition, you should start by organizing your thoughts (see *Sorting Out the Story* for ideas). Since the Web allows for much more than just words on a page, you should also begin to think about how graphics, sound, video, or animation could help you tell your story better or in different ways. To organize all of the elements of a Web site, you should begin by drawing a rough sketch of all the pages within

the site. A sketch of how your Web pages will look and relate to one another in sequence is called a *storyboard*.

Sorting Out the Story

★ Chronological: Let visitors to your site follow your adventure day-by-day as in Figure 9.6.

★ Unique Things I Saw: Include a link to the most interesting and important things you saw on your trip as in Figure 9.7.

★ Friends I Made: Introduce the world to the people you met along your way.

When you are describing where you went, it might help to include a map or two. There are lots of places to get maps on the Web, or you can draw your own (using a computer program or by hand). Maps are instructive and can be really fun both to create and to see—check out *Mapping It Out* in Chapter 5 for help and more information.

3. Turn your storyboard into a real Web site.

Publishing the story of your journey can be complicated. Make sure you have all the necessary tools to make the design and implementation of your Web site as smooth as possible (look at the beginning of this chapter for a list of tools).When you have revised and proofread your site, post your work on a Web server. You may need to contact your local Internet service provider or ask for advice online when you go to put your site up.

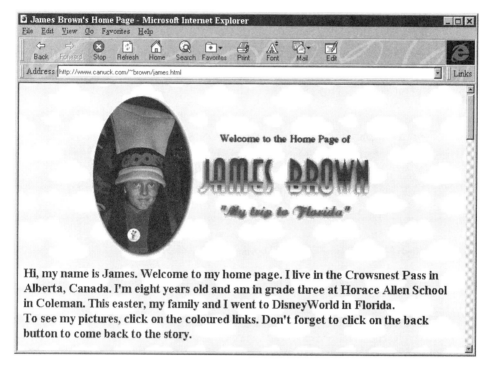

FIGURE 9.6: Follow James Brown through his three excellent days in Florida—an example of a chronological organization (`http://www.canuck.com/~brown/james.html`).

TIP

A picture is worth a thousand words. Unfortunately, not all of us have access to digital cameras for taking Web-ready pictures. So if you're looking for pictures to illustrate your travel journal, look around the Web for pictures to use (don't forget to ask permission before you post them on your site). Most newer browsers have a "Save As" function, so you should be able to download the pictures directly and then use them in your Adventure site.

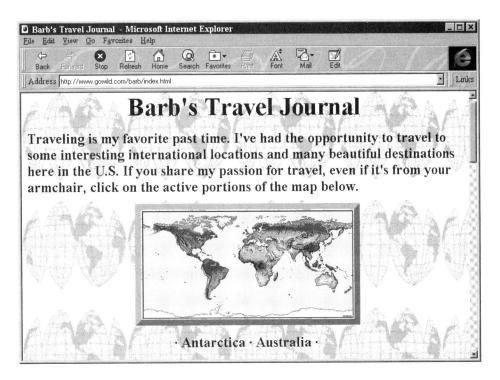

FIGURE 9.7: **Barb's Travel Journal brings you insights on a variety of topics related to her travels in Antarctica** (`http://www.gowild.com/barb/index.html`).

4. Invite others to take your journey.

Having not only traveled great (or not so great) distances to get the story and then worked so hard to publish your tale on the Web, you will want others to see your site. Contact related sites (check out the sites listed below for some sites that might be similar to yours) and ask the Webmaster to make a link to you.

HOT! HOT! HOT!

NOVA Online: Alive on Everest
http://www.pbs.org/wgbh/pages/nova/everest

NOVA, the popular science show on PBS, sent a team of climbers to attempt the highest peak in the world, Mount Everest. The expedition is over, but the daily updates, photos, history, and virtual reality are still there to amaze you.

Adventure Online: Guide to Adventure Learning
http://www.adventureonline.com

Tag along on trips to Greenland, Central America, and Africa. Also, you can climb the highest peak in the United States, Mount McKinley, with cancer survivors.

MayaQuest
http://www.mecc.com/internet/maya/maya.html

Here you can follow the travels of a team of adventurers in Mexico, Guatemala, and Belize as they seek out the lost civilization of the Mayan people. You can help them make important decisions about what they will do and where they will go by voting online!

TerraQuest
http://www.terraquest.com/index.html

Virtual adventure abounds here. Take a trip to the Galapagos Islands, climb Yosemite National Park's El Capitan, or visit the Antarctic.

Discovery Online: Exploration
http://www.discovery.com/area/exploration/exploration.html

Discovery Online hosts several live, ongoing virtual journeys every month. Updated daily, these travel journals bring you vivid photography and opportunities to ask questions and interact with the travelers.

Appendix A

Resources

This appendix is a resource guide to the Internet sources you will find throughout the book, along with a few others we thought were useful. The resources are alphabetized by name under the following categories:

> **Art and Music**
> **Fun and Games**
> **Geography and Environment**
> **Government**
> **History**
> **Literature and Writing**
> **Mathematics**
> **Miscellaneous**
> **Net Tools**
> **News and E-Zines**
> **Parent Resources**
> **Reference**
> **Science and Health**
> **Search Tools**
> **Sports and Hobbies**

Art and Music

Allmusic

This listserv offers discussion on all forms of music. Topics include composition, musicology, jazz, classical, funk, acoustics, and performance.

Subscribe to: listserv@american.edu

All Star Magazine

Musicians of all shapes and sizes are addressed in the pages of *All Star Magazine*.

http://allstarmag.com/news

Alt.music.lyrics

A Usenet group for songwriters and anyone else interested in discussing song lyrics.

subscribe to: alt.music.lyrics

America's Shrine to Music Museum

This site takes you on a virtual tour of a South Dakota museum, which houses more than 6,000 instruments from all over the world.

http://www.usd.edu.smm

AMG All-Music Guide

This is a complete online database of recorded music. Just type in an artist, album, or song title and get more information than you thought imaginable!

http://allmovie.com/amg/music_root.html

ArtsEdNet

Although this site is designed primarily for art teachers, it provides a large collection of online images of artworks.

http://www.artsednet.getty.edu

ArtsWire

Search the "WebBase" at ArtsWire to find all kinds of information about an area of fine arts such as dance, theater, sculpture and painting.

http://www.artswire.org

Chicks Rock

This site is dedicated to women rockers and includes interviews, artists, new bands, books, and essays.

http://www.media.ku.dk/students/anya/CHICKS.htm

CyberKids/CyberTeens Young Composers

If you really get the composing bug, find some like-minded friends at this site.

http://www.cyberkids.com/composers/composers.html

The Grammy Music Awards

This is home to the music awards show on the Web.

http://www.grammy.com

Guitar Instruction

Everything you want to know about playing the guitar can be found there. This site even includes an online guitar lesson.

```
http://www.scott.net/~mwarren/noframes/instruction.html
```

Harmony Central

The Massachusetts Institute of Technology (MIT) offers a great collection of MIDI tidbits.

```
http://harmony-central.com
```

Internet Underground Music Archive

This is a music archive for all kinds of bands and musicians that are relatively unknown.

```
http://www.iuma.com
```

WNUR-FM JazzWeb Information Server

Sponsored by Northwestern University since 1993, this site contains loads of information about jazz music, musicians, history, education, and performances.

```
http://www.nwu.edu/WNUR/jazz
```

Latin Music On-Line!

If you like Luis Miguel, you'll love this site!

```
http://www.lamusica.com
```

Library of Congress Vatican Exhibit

From the main hall, you can choose which room you would like to explore. Rooms such as "Archeology," "Mathematics," and "Orient to Rome" house images of original documents that can only be seen at the Vatican, home of the Pope and the Catholic Church.

```
http://sunsite.unc.edu/expo/vatican.exhibit/exhibit/Main_
Hall.html
```

The Lyrics Library

This site provides all kinds of lyrical resources.

```
http://web2.kw.igs.net/~wgarvin.lyrics.welcome.html
```

The MIDI Home Page

In addition to a long list of additional MIDI sites, you can get an introduction to MIDI here.

```
http://www.eeb.ele.tue.nl/midi/index.html
```

Movies Discussion

This is a Usenet group that contains discussions about movies.

Subscribe to: `rec.arts.movies`

Musi-Cal

This is a gateway to live music.

```
http://concerts.calendar.com
```

Music Previews Network

Here you can read reviews and sample sound clips from artists in all genres of music.

http://www.previews.net

MTV

The online companion to the popular cable channel is devoted to popular music and music news.

http://www.mtv.com

National Museum of American Art

A fantastic place to visit to see the latest online exhibitions, consult the Museum's online journal, *American Art*, or even pose a question at the online reference desk.

http://www.nmaa.si.edu

The Oscars

Want to know the nominations and winners of the Academy Awards? Go to the official site of the Academy of Motion Picture Arts & Sciences.

http://www.oscars.org/ampas

SITO

This is a place for image-makers and image-lovers to exchange ideas, collarborate and meet.

http://www.sito.org

The Piano Education Page

You'll find tips on learning to play the piano, getting the right kind of piano lessons and piano teacher, piano-teaching software, links to other piano and music-related sites, interviews, and a special page for kids.

`http://www.unm.edu/~loritaf/pnoedmn.html`

rec.music.a-cappella

This is a Usenet group for those who enjoy performing or listening to a cappella (voice-only) music.

Subscribe to: `rec.music.a-cappella`

rec.music.compose

This is a Usenet group with discussion about notation and composition software, sources of inspiration, getting published, book reviews, and computer hardware used in composition.

Subscribe to: `rec.music.compose`

rec.music.info

This is a Usenet group with information about music resources on the Internet: FTP sites, music newsgroups, mailing lists, discographies, concert dates, chart listings, and new releases.

Subscribe to: `rec.music.info`

rec.music.makers.percussion

This a Usenet group with discussions about percussion instruments.

Subscribe to: `rec.music.makers.percussion`

Rock and Roll Hall of Fame

The legends of rock are here at the virtual hall of fame.

http://www.rockhall.com

Smithsonian Online

There are 11 Smithsonian museums in Washington, D.C., which can be explored from this site. You can visit one museum directly, explore all of them through categories, or even search all of the museums for what interests you.

http://www.si.edu

Web Museum, Paris

This site houses a large collection of artwork found in Paris museums from many artistic styles and eras such as the Renaissance, Impressionism, and Contemporary.

http://www.amazed.hl/wm

World Band

This is a project involving a set of schools whose students are using MIDI synthesizer and computer sequencing software.

http://conect.bbn.com/WorldBand/CoNECTMusic.html

Worldwide Internet Music Resources

This site is your ticket to finding all kinds of musical information. Everything from links to sites for specific artists, to sites about different types of music, to links for musical journals and magazines.

http://music.indiana.edu/music_resources

Fun and Games

Acekids

The Academic Center for Excellence (ACE) sponsors several contests such as brain teasers and poetry writing.

http://www.acekids.com/games.html

Adventure

Feel the spirit of adventure as you explore the Colossal Caves, seeking adventure and warding off hostile characters. This a text-based fantasy adventure that is now available through the Web.

http://www-tjww.stanford.edu/adventure

Afro-Americ@ Kids Zone

This site contains brain teasers and informative trivia games.

http://www.afroam.org/children/children.html

Board Games

A site where you can play backgammon, chess, Go (a Korean game), Scrabble, and XiangQi (Chinese chess).

http://alabanza.com/kabacoff/Inter-Links/fun/b_games.html

Bonus.com

A site where you can play games and win prizes.

http://www.bonus.com

Cyber Kids

This site is a free online magazine that contains stories and artwork by and for kids.

http://www.mtlake.com/cyberkids

Cyberarts

This is an amazing backgammon site that allows anyone to set up an account and play for one hour per day without charge. For serious enthusiasts who want to obtain a skill rating and play more than one hour per day, a fee-based subscription is necessary. You will need to download a small program that lets you run this online backgammon game.

http://www.cyberarts.com

Cyberkids

This site contains a reading room and art gallery as well as games.

http://www.cyberkids.com

CyberSurfari

This site features an annual contest that is like a treasure hunt, but on the Internet!

http://www.spa.org/cybersurfari

Develcor

Includes games such as Battleship, Checkers, and so on that can be downloaded and then played against other people online, or against your own computer.

http://www.develcor.com

Disneyland/Disneyworld

Everything you wanted to know about these world famous places for fun and magic is found at this site. Mickey always rolls out the red carpet for his guests!

`http://www.disney.com`

Diversity University

This site, designed to be a virtual university, is a fun place in cyberspace.

`http://www.du.org`

Dr. Bowen's Incredible Contest Club

If you're looking for contests, look no further than Dr. Bowen's Club.

`http://www.contestclub.com`

Earth Dog Contest

The Earth Dog is a sort of environmental superhero. You can enter the essay contest from this site. You can even win a WebTV terminal.

`http://www.earthdog.com`

Freezone

This is a wild site with lots of fun stuff to do including contests that you can win!

`http://freezone.com`

Fundrum My Conundrum

Great site for different levels of difficulty of riddles. The only drawback is that you have to send $12 for the answers.

http://www.cataloguesonline.com/puzzles

Funstuff

This site, provided by GTE laboratories, includes Web games of Battleship, Minesweeper, Rubik's Magic Cube, and A Virtual Maze.

http://info.gte.com/gtel/fun

Games Domain

Here at the Games Domain, you can read games reviews, download games, and enter contests. You can even get cool graphics for your Web page.

http://www.gamesdomain.com/tigger/swkids.html

GeoCities Enchanted Forest

The Enchanted Forest is an area of the Web staked out by pioneering kids. Add your page or simply visit the pages put up by other kids.

http://www.geocities.com/EnchantedForest

Happy Puppy Kidz Page

A site containing free games from brain teasers to 3-D action games.

http://www.happypuppy.com/kids

Java on the Brain

A site of one person's collection of games developed with the Java programming language.

http://www.tdb.uu.se/~karl/brain.html

KidLinks

This site links Web pages from kids younger than the age of 13.

http://www.geocities.com/CaptitolHill/3261/kidlinks.html

KidStation

This site takes the pulse of kids today by posing topical questions each week.

http://www.ingenius.com/kids/poll.htm

Kids' Place in Space

Sponsored by Virgin Entertainment, this site offers a monthly contest and gives out free software to winners!

http://www.vsv.com/kidship/index.html

Kinglink Games

There are many different types of games here, though be sure not to miss Dino Numbers and Dino Spell, two games that will improve your math and spelling skills while you have fun.

http://www.kinglink.com/gameforum.html

Loteria

A Web site where you can play a Mexican game like Bingo that uses pictures rather than numbers.

http://www.mercado.com/juventud/loteria/loteria.htm

MaMaMedia

This site has games and other neat things for kids and it allows you to create your own Web page using sound and pictures they provide.

http://mamamedia.com

Mike Rofoni, Roving Reporter

Mike Rofoni is a reporter who happens also to be a walking microphone. That aside, this is fun, on-going story that you can explore as you wish.

http://www.indigo.ie/local/mikero/contents.html

Movie Makers Guild

Learn how to create storyboards that are the road map for the hit movie you now have in your head. Real movie makers share ideas and ask for your help at this site.

http://www.el-dorado.co.us/~dmnews/mmguild.html

The NoodleHead Network

Sponsored by an award-winning video company that creates videos from a kid's eye view, this site takes you through the different phases of making a video using a basic camcorder.

http://www.noodlehead.com/about/about.html

PlaySite

A site where you can challenge someone to a game of chess, checkers, reversi, or backgammon.

http://www.playsite.com

ThinkQuest

Check out this online contest for schools, classes, and individual students.

http://www.advanced.org/thinkquest

Tic Tac Toe

A site where you can play Tic Tac Toe.

http://netpressence.com/npchi.ttt

Too Cool for Grownups

A highly interactive site with games, stories, Web projects, and a listing of top Web sites. This site also conducts a poll on what's hot and what's not.

http://www.tcfg.com

Visa Olympics of the Imagination

Be sure to click on "Special Events" to get to the contests.

http://www.visa.com/cgi-bin/vee/ev/voi/main.html?2+0

Web Mine Sweeper

To make your way through this minefield, you will have to use your head.

http://info.gte.com/gtel/fun/mines/mines.html

WWW 4 kidz Weekly Contests

This site offers activities, games, and contests for kids.

`http://www.4kidz.com`

The Yuckiest Site on the Internet

Explore all the gross things in the world and have a good time doing it.

`http://www.nj.com/yucky`

Zarf's Ex-List of Interactive Games

Games, games, games! Everything from Tic Tac Toe to trivia.

`http://www.leftfoot.com/realgames.html#games`

Geography and Environment

Adventure Online

This site follows adventure trips around the world.

`http://www.adventureonline.com`

The Adventure WebRing

The WebRing links together lots of terrific tales of adventure, travel, and discovery.

`http://www.realkids.com/webring.htm`

Atlapedia Online

`http://www.atlapedia.com`

This site contains profiles of every county from A to Z.

Barb's Travel Journal

This site tracks Barb on her trips to places like Antarctica.

http://www.gowild.com/barb/index.html

CoVis: Learning through Collaborative Visualization

Here you can check out scientists sharing information and expertise on the Internet.

http://www.covis.nwu.edu

Discovery Channel Online: Exploration

With expeditions going on all the time, Discovery brings you along expeditions in search of dinosaurs, elephants, sharks, and much more.

http://www.discovery.com

Earth Day

This site can serve as your Earth Day headquarters.

http://www.envirolink.org/earthday

Environmental Protection Agency's Web Site for Students and Teachers

Find facts about the environment as well as links to other environmental sites on the Web. Facts are organized around current issues such as clean air, hazardous waste and ozone depletion.

http://www.epa.gov/epahome/students.htm

Expedia

To find the best restaurant or the museum's hours, check out Expedia.

`http://www.expedia.msn.com/wg`

The GeoNet Game

`http://www.hmco.com/hmco/school/geo/indexhi.thml`

This is a game where you think and learn geographically.

Global Land Information

A Telnet site with detailed geographical information.

`telnet://glis.cr.usgs.gov`

Global Online Adventure Learning Site (GOALS)

Dedicated to online learning, GOALS is also full of the spirit of adventure on such trips as a rowing expedition around the world and three young brothers on a two-year sailing trip around the Pacific Ocean.

`http://www.adventureonline.com/other/goals.html`

The Great Globe Gallery

This site has a lot of graphics of globes and maps including a satellite image of the earth.

`http://hum.amu.edu.pl/~zbzw/glob/glob0.htm`

Heritage Map Museum

This site has maps from hundreds of years ago.

`http://www.carto.com/index.htm`

Historical Maps of the United States

This University of Texas collection of maps makes a great resource for learning about the history of the USA. Check out maps that show Native American population and European settlement and expansion through time. Plus, city maps!

http://www.lib.utexas.edu/Libs/PCL/Map_collection/histus.html

International Kids' Space

This site posts kids' writing, art, and music.

http://www.interport.net/kids-space

James Brown

This site tells you everything you ever wanted to know about young James Brown's vacation to Disneyworld.

http://www.canuck.com/~brown/james.html

JASON Project

This project was started by the scientist who discovered the Titanic, Dr. Robert D. Ballard, because he received so many letters from students asking how he made his discovery. Each year students around the country join scientists on a variety of adventures through computer communication and satellite links.

http://www.jasonproject.org

Lonely Planet Travel Guides

Read the comprehensive travel guides, get in touch with other travelers, even add your two cents to the guide books or send a multimedia postcard.

http://www.lonelyplanet.com

Mapquest

This site offers maps from all over the world.

http://www.mapquest.com

MayaQuest

This site follows the adventures of a group of intrepid travelers in search of the lost civilization of Central America's Maya people.

http://www.mecc.com/mayaquest.html

The National Park Service

Whether you want to relive a prior trip to a national park or plan a future one, this site has all you need to know. Learn about the wildlife, the environment, and what trails or camping sites are available for you to experience the great outdoors!

http://www.nps.gov

NOVA Online: Alive on Everest

Here you can feel like you're climbing Everest alongside some of the world's greatest mountaineers.

http://www.pbs.org/wgbh/pages/nova/everest

TerraQuest

This site is devoted to virtual trips to a variety of exotic places.

http://www.terraquest.com/index.html

TraveloCity

Be sure to click on Destinations and Interests to find a spot in the world to visit.

http://www.travelocity.com

University of Iowa, Center for Global & Regional Environmental Research

One aspect of environmental research is the need to create and update maps for many different outdoor locations. Thanks to the University of Iowa you get to see them too on the Web!

http://www.cgrer.uiowa.edu/servers/servers-reference.html

Virtual Voyager

Travel to the depths of the oceans or to the heights of outer space.

http://www.chron.com/voyager/index.html

Government

The Blacksburg, Virginia Electronic Village

This site documents the civic and cultural life of one of the most wired towns in America.

http://www.bev.net

CapWeb, A Guide to the U.S. Congress

This site provides a way to learn more about what's happening on Capitol Hill.

```
http://policy.net/capweb/congress.html
```

Government Information Locator

A site where you can search for mailing addresses and information about the people of the federal government.

```
http://www.law.vill.edu/fed-agency/fedwebloc.html
```

Legislate Gopher Service

This site contains bills and other documents relating to the current session of the U.S. Congress.

```
gopher://gopher.legislate.com
```

Our Town

This site, created by the Computer Learning Foundation, helps communities and individuals make their presence felt on the Web.

```
http://www.tcfn.org/ourtown.htm
```

Politicians' E-mail Adresses

On this site, you can search for governmental e-mail addresses.

```
http://webcom.com/~leavitt/cong.html
```

USA CityLink

This site gives a comprehensive listing of U.S. states and cities that provide information on the Web.

```
http://www.usacitylink.com/visitcity.html
```

White House for Kids

Take a tour of the White House and meet its occupants.

```
http://www.whitehouse.gov/WH/kids/html/home.html
```

Youth in Action

This site has a monthly on youth-related issues.

```
http://www.mightymedia.com/act/tools/noise/noise.cfm
```

History

The History Channel

```
http://www.historychannel.com
```

On this site you can read famous speeches from history, or you can check out "This Day in History."

HNSource

This site offers access to historical events and documents.

```
telnet://ukanaix.cc.ukans.edu
```

Library of Congress, American Memory

This site goes to the main Library of Congress page. From here, you can go to the American Memory page, as well as a lot of other great resources.

`http://lcweb.loc.gov`

USA Government & Historical Resources

This site contains links to other Web pages about history and government. You can find the Virtual Reference Desk under the link to "Politics and Government."

`http://gopher.libraries.wayne.edu`

Literature and Writing

Ask the Author

The Internet Public Library has enlisted a group of youth authors and illustrators to answer your questions about literature.

`http://www.ipl.org/youth/AskAuthor/AskAuthor.html`

The Bartleby Project

Here you can access a wide variety of complete literary works.

`http://www.columbia.edu/acis/bartleby`

Bookwire

Here you can find lots of stuff on books and their authors.

`http://www.bookwire.com`

A Celebration of Women Writers

This site contains works written by and about women authors.

http://almond.srv.cs.cmu.edu/afs/cs.cmu.edu/user/mmbt/www/
women/celebration.html

The Children and Young Adult
Writing Workshop Listserv

Talking with actual authors of children and young adult books might help you join the ranks of authors. Use this listserv to pose questions and learn from today's authors.

Subscribe to: yawrite@lists.psu.edu

Children's Writings

This is a fantastic source for really good kids' writing. Use it for inspiration and entertainment or as a place to get yourself published.

http://www.ucalgary.ca/~dkbrown/writings.html

Classic Short Stories

Dedicated to the American short story, this site offers many stories and opportunities to post your own.

http://www.bnl.com/shorts

Cloak and Dagger Fiction Unlimited

This is a great place to visit for good fiction written by two young people who are fascinated by gargoyles, dragons, and aliens.

http://www.mindspring.com/~cloak_and_dagger

Folk Tales Set in Africa

This site contains folk tales written by a group of American students with some help from mentors from Africa that they met through the Internet.

http://hi-c.eecs.umich.edu/umdl/stories97

Gutenberg Project

This project aims to make the world's great works of literature available for free over the Internet.

http://promo.net/pg

Inklings

Besides serving as a resource for young writers, the Inkspot publishes a nifty lit zine, called *Inklings*.

http://www.inkspot.com/inklings

The Inkspot

The Inkspot's Resources for Young Writers offers lots of advice for getting your work published.

http://www.inkspot.com/young

The Inkwell

This site serves as a showcase for poetry written by a 16-year-old aspiring poet. Good stuff!

http://www.geocities.com/SoHo/5249

The Internet Poetry Archive

Here you can read poetry from selected modern poets.

```
http://sunsite.unc.edu/dykki/poetry/home.html
```

The Internet Public Library

Just like your local public library but online.

```
http://www.ipsl.org
```

The Looking Glass Gazette

Written and published by kids, the focus of this publication is stories, poems, and artwork created by kids 13 years of age and younger.

```
http://www.cowboy.net/~mharper/LGG.html
```

Poet's Corner

This is a project that provides students with a place to publish their poetry and have an audience that will respond and give feedback to them. Poetic forums are provided throughout the year that may serve as "springboards" for writing.

```
http://pen1.pen.k12.va.us/Anthology/Pav/LangArts/
poetcorner.html
```

Project Eris

If you enjoy reading from your computer screen, this is the Gopher site for you, with dozens of classic texts—all in fast-loading, plain-vanilla text.

```
gopher://gopher.vt.edu:10010/10/33
```

Purdue University's Writing Lab

This site provides a guide to citing references found on the Internet.

`http://owl.trc.purdue.edu/files/110.html`

The View from My Window

Here students from all over describe what they see out their windows. It seems like a simple thing to do, but the responses are sometimes beautiful and poetic.

`http://www.youth.net/window/hypermail/index.html`

A Vision

An I*EARN project, this literary magazine publishes art, poetry, and prose created by secondary school students from all over the world.

`http://www.igc.apc.org/iearn/projects/av.html`

The Vocal Point

Written collaboratively by middle school students all over the United States, *Vocal Point* tackles a new topic in each issue.

`http://bvsd.k12.co.us/cent/Newspaper/Newspaper.html`

The Young Author's Workshop

The purpose of this site is to provide middle school students with links to online resources that takes visitors through the writing process, step by step.

`http://www.planet.eon.net/~bplaroch/index.html`

Mathematics

Ask Dr. Math

Whether you are in elementary, middle, high school, or even college you can send your math question to Dr. Math and get help with it. Check the archives first and then send your question to the doctor.

http://forum.swarthmore.edu/dr.math/dr-math.html

The Math Forum

In addition to new fun ways to look at mathematical puzzles, this site provides all kinds of information about all kinds of math.

http://forum.swarthmore.edu/index.html

MathMagic!

This site posts challenges in each of four grade categories (K-3, 4-6, 7-9, 10-12) and encourages each registered team to pair up with another team to solve the challenge.

http://forum.swarthmore.edu/mathmagic

Biographies of Women Mathematicians

These pages are part of an on-going project by students in mathematics classes at Agnes Scott College in Atlanta, Georgia, to illustrate the numerous achievements of women in the field of mathematics.

http://www.scottlan.edu/lriddle/women/women.html

MEGA Mathematics

Mathematics is a live science with new discoveries being made every day. Check out this site to play and experiment with new ideas.

`http://www.c3.lanl.gov:80/mega-math`

Miscellaneous

American Girl

This is an online club for girls with neat ideas, places to talk and interesting articles.

`http://www.americangirl.com/ag/ag.cgi`

Ask an Expert

This site advertises "Free advice from the Amish to zoo keeping!" You can select from 12 categories with more than 300 Web sites and e-mail addresses where you can find experts to answer your questions.

`http://www.askanexpert.com/askanexpert`

Ask Ken!

You may not know who Ken is, but some people think he is the "Dear Abby" of the Web.

`http://www.efn.org/~andrec/ask_ken.html`

Adam Jones for President in 2024

Look for Adam Jones to run for president as soon as he is old enough!

`http://www.mich.com/~jones`

Alice's Home Page

This is a home page created by an English girl named Alice.

```
http://www.comlab.ox.ac.uk/oucl/users/jonathan.bowen/
children/alice.html
```

Camila's Home Page

This home page was created by a Nicaraguan girl named Camila.

```
http://www.uca.edu.ni/~sergio/camila.html
```

Keisuke's Home Page

This is a site where a Japanese girl named Keisuke shows her art on her own home page.

```
http://www.tama.or.jp/~adeu/keisuke/index.html
```

Kids Connect

```
http://www.ala.org/ICONN/kidsconn.html
```

A questions and answer service for helping kids online do research for school projects.

Melrose School

This site includes drawings and stories by students at the Melrose School in Oakland, California.

```
http://ousd.k12.ca.us/melrose
```

Monika's Home Page

This is a home page created by a girl name Monika.

```
http://www.whidbey.net/~irvbough/live.htm
```

New Jersey's Ask An Expert Page

Although this site is supported by New Jersey businesses, anyone on the Internet can use the service that categorizes experts by categories.

```
http://njnie.dl.stevens-tech.edu/curriculum/aska.html
```

Nobel Prize Awards

Check in to see who will win this year's Nobel prizes.

```
http://www.almaz.com/nobel
```

Oakland Unified School District

This site contains information on the school district and links to individual schools in the district.

```
http://ousd.k12.ca.us
```

Pen Pal Planet

Make friends, learn about other cultures, and even improve your writing by exchanging snail mail letters with a pen pal. At this site you can get started, provided you are between 12 and 20 years old.

```
http://www.epix.net/~ppplanet/page7.html
```

SeaWorld/Busch Gardens Animal Information Database

```
http://www.seaworld.org
```

Go to this site to see and learn about 32 sharks through the shark cam.

Net Tools

A Beginner's Guide to HTML

Learn the basics of HTML programming for the Web on this site.

`http://www.ncsa/uiuc.edu/General/Internet/WWW/HTMLPrimer.html`

Beginner's Guide to HTML

This site will tell you all that you need to know to begin building Web pages.

`http://www.gnn.com/gnn/wic.html.03.html`

Claris Home Page

Go to this site to learn more about this company's HTML editing tool.

`http://www.claris.com`

Comtouch

This site provides e-mail software that allows you to include graphics.

`http://www.comtouch.com`

Create Your Own

Here you'll find a guide to creating your own Web site.

`http://www.smplanet.com/webpage/webpage.html`

Hotmail

For free e-mail, check out this site.

`http://www.hotmail.com`

Hot Dog Express

This is a fantastic place to start when you are learning how to do HTML editing.

`http://www.sausage.com`

HTML Land

This site has lots of good information on Web publishing.

`http://cygnus.campbellsvil.edu/~chgibbs/html.html`

HTML Writer

This site will help you create your own Web pages.

`http://www.public.asu.edu/~bottger`

HyperStudio

A popular program that many kids use at school to develop multimedia reports and now, even school home pages.

`http://www.hyperstudio.com`

Intermind

When you become a member of Intermind (which is free) you can select the "channels" (Web sites) that you frequent the most and they come up on your own page. You will also be informed when a site is updated with new information.

`http://www.intermind.com`

Internet Safety

Everything you need to know to be "Web safe."

`http://www.uoknor.edu/oupd/kidsafe/inet.htm`

Liszt, the Mailing List Directory

This Web site has a listing of all the listservs available to you. You can even search for the area of your interest.

`http://www.liszt.com`

Microsoft FrontPage & Word 97

This well-known publisher of software produces an HTML editor called FrontPage as well as allowing Word documents to be saved as HTML.

`http://www.microsoft.com/products`

Microsoft Internet Explorer

Internet Explorer is one of the most popular browsers for the Web.

`http://www.microsoft.com/products`

Netscape Communicator

Netscape made the first browser for the Web and continues to improve it with new versions. Version 4.0 is the newest.

`http://www.netscape.com`

PageMill

Published by Adobe, this is a popular HTML editor to make your pages look the way you want.

`http://www.adobe.com/prodindex/pagemill/main.html`

Qualcomm

If you use Eudora as your e-mail software, Qualcomm's site may be of interest to you. Qualcomm is the publisher of the software and can help with any technical questions you may have.

```
http://www.qualcomm.com
```

Search for Listservs

Here you can search for listservs by topic or by name.

```
http://catalog.com/vivian/interest-group-search.html
```

Internet Service Providers

This site contains information about ISPs.

```
http://www.tagonline.com/Providers
```

Internet Tutorial

This "Netiquette" resource, from Microsoft, will teach you lots about the Internet and how to use it.

```
http://www.msn.com/tutorial/default.html
```

McAfee's VirusScan

Download a trial version of McAfee's VirusScan to guard against those pesky programs that can wreak havoc on your machine and files.

```
http://www.mcafee.com
```

Norton Anti-Virus

Download a trial version of Norton's virus scanner to guard against those pesky programs that can wreak havoc on your computer and files.

http://www.norton.com

K.I.D.S.

This is similar to the Scout Report, but it is produced bimonthly by kids, for kids. It is an ongoing, cooperative effort of two classrooms in Boulder, CO, and Madison, WI.

http://wwwscout.cs.wisc.edu/scout/KIDS

PointCast

This company provides you with free software to download that lets you have your very own news station on the Internet! Throughout the day you can get up-to-the-minute news.

http://www.redcreek.net/pointcast.htm

Prodigy Internet

This Internet service provider (ISP) lets you customize your gateway to the Internet based on your interests and needs.

http://www.prodigy.com

The Scout Report

Published every Friday both on the Web and by e-mail, it provides a fast, convenient way to stay informed of valuable resources on the Internet.

http://www.scout.cs.wisc.edu

TUCOWS

`http://www.tucows.com`

Here you can download a variety of Internet resources.

Web 66

This site provides links to schools' Web sites and includes several links to sample appropriate use documents.

`http://mustang.coled.umn.edu/Started/use/Acceptableuse.html`

News and E-Zines

ABC News

This is the online component of ABC's television news coverage.

`http://www.abcnews.com`

Afro-Americ@News

Every week, this site compiles the top news stories affecting African-Americans across the country.

`http://www.afroam.org`

Aboriginal Youth Network, News Center

In Australia, there are many youth from the aboriginal (or native) tribes. This is a place where news affecting their lives is collected and available.

`http://ayn-0.ayn.ca/PAGES/news.htm`

Cable News Network (CNN)

The 24-hour news network CNN is now on the Web.

http://www.cnn.com

Children's Express

This site is a news service produced by kids reporting on the issues that affect their lives.

http://www.ce.org

ClariNet

ClariNet provides the broadest, up-to-the-minute news coverage on the Internet, with more than 3,500 stories per day from major news wires, and continuous updates around the clock.

http://www.clarient.com/single/internet.html

C-SPAN Online

http://www.c-span.org

This is a 24-hour a day news site that will keep you up-to-date on happenings in the world.

CyberKids

This is a cool place for kids to hang out and have fun. There is a free online magazine that contains stories and artwork created by kids.

http://www.mtlake.com/cyberkids

GLC Online!

This newsletter is created by the youth of Loraine, IL, and includes stories, polls, and poetry.

http://www.geocities.com/Athens/4582/glc01.html

Global Show-n-Tell

This virtual exhibition lets kids show off their favorite projects, possessions, accomplishments, and collections to other kids around the world.

http://www.manymedia.com/show-n-tell

InfiNet Newsstand

Look here to find an online newspaper from the many that InfiNet operates around the country.

http://www.infi.net/newsstand.html

Internet Relay Chat

A Usenet group discusses how to use IRC.

Subscribe to: alt.irc

The Irish Times

Get all the latest news and weather across Ireland.

http://www.irish-times.ie

Jr. Seahawk News

One middle school's approach to putting their newspaper on the Web.

http://www.halcyon.com/arborhts/jrseahaw.html

Junior High School Students Discussion

A Usenet group for middle school students to discuss whatever is on their minds.

`k12.chat.junior`

Kidlink

Kidlink is a project to get kids aged 10–15 involved in a global dialog, through a fun Web site, activities, and a newsletter.

`http://www.kidlink.org/english/index.html`

Kidlink

This listserv is a place for you to get together and share ideas and experiences with other kids.

Subscribe to: `listservr@nodak.edu`

KidNews

This is an online news and writing service for students and teachers around the world. Anyone may use stories from the service for educational purposes, and anyone may submit stories.

`http://www.kidnews.com`

KidPub

This site help kids publish anything they want on the Web.

`http://www.kidpub.org`

KidsCare

Check out this site to see an online newsletter in action.

`http://kidscare.org`

Kidsphere

Use this listserv to meet kids your age from all over the world.

Subscribe to: `kidsphere@vms.cis.pitt.edu`

MidLink Magazine

This e-zine is written by kids and for kids in middle school, and it is an award-winning showcase for young creative writers.

`http://longwood.cs.ucf.edu/~MidLink`

Mighty Media KeyPals Club

This site contains a poll with a question that changes every month.

`http://www.mightymedia.com`

MSNBC

This shares the news from Microsoft and NBC news.

`http://www.msnbc.com`

The New York Times

The motto of this newspaper is "All the news that's fit to print." With the Internet, they've found a new way to print... electronically!

`http://www.nytimes.com`

Pathfinder

This is the Web site for Time Warner, the publisher of magazines such as *Sports Illustrated*, *Time*, and *Entertainment Weekly*.

`http://www.pathfinder.com/kids`

Pen-pals

This listserv helps people to find Net pals.

Subscribe to: `pen-pals-request@mainstream.com`

Spanish Speaking Kids Discussion

This is a Usenet group where you can talk to kids around the world and practice your Spanish.

`k12.lang.esp-eng`

The Surfrider

The Surfrider is a great example of bringing a school's newspaper on the Web.

`http://www.pixi.com/~kailuah2/surfrider`

Top News

This is a service of Lycos, a popular search tool, that provides a great array of top news stories.

`http://www.topnews.com`

United Nations Youth Information Network

The Youth Information Network is a project of the United Nations to track issues related to youth around the world.

`http://www.un.org/dpcsd/dspd/unyin.htm`

USA Today

Check this site for the Web version of this popular daily newspaper that covers the United States.

http://www.usatoday.com/usafront.htm

Voices of Youth

This site, part of UNICEF, provides information on the United Nations Children's Fund.

http://www.unicef.org/voy

The Washington Post Online

Known for its political coverage, this venerable newspaper is now completely online.

http://www.washingtonpost.com

Youth Net

This site provides access to information of interest to young people.

http://www.youth.net

Parent Resources

CyberPatrol

This site provides information about a piece of software for filtering and monitoring the Internet.

http://www.microsys.com/cyber/default.htm

Guide to Internet Parenting from Voters Telecommunications Watch

This site contains important information for parents whose kids use the Web.

http://www.vtw.org/parents

FamilyPC

This site asks kids and parent to review Web sites.

http://www.cybertours.com/yccs/survey/html

The Librarians Guide to Cyberspace for Parents and Kids

This site has ideas from librarians for parents and their kids.

http://www.ala.org/parents

NetNanny

This site provides information about a piece of software that monitors a child's use of the Internet.

http://www.netnanny.com

Parents' Guide to the Information Super Highway

This site is a parent's guide to the Web.

http://www.childrenspartnership.org

ParentsPlace.com

Learn more about the Web and share ideas with other parents.

http://www.parentsplace.com

Surfwatch

This site explains a software application that monitors your child's use of the Internet.

http://www.surfwatch.com

Reference

Atlapedia Online

http://www.atlapedia.com

This site contains profiles of every county from A to Z.

Cyberatlas

Cyberatlas tracks demographic and other statistical data relating to use of the Internet.

http://www.cyberatlas.com

Education Gopher at Florida Tech

This Gopher site has lots of plain-text educational resources, including a super-fast "reference desk" with dictionary and thesaurus.

gopher://sci-ed.fit.edu

My Virtual Reference Desk

This is an amazing collection of reference resources such as the Webster's Dictionary, encyclopedias, atlases, weather, and others in many other subject areas. This site is bound to have a resource that can help you answer your question.

http://www.refdesk.com

World Factbook

This site is maintained by the CIA and includes detailed information about locations around the world.

http://cliffie.nosc.mil/~NATLAS/wfb/index.html

Science and Health

Ability OnLine Support Network

Connect to young people with disabilities or chronic illnesses.

http://www.ablelink.org

Ask a High-Energy Astronomer

Have questions about X-rays or gamma ray astronomy? Go here!

http://asca.gsfc.nasa.gov/docs/learning_center/ask_astro/
ask_an_astronomer.html

Ask a Scientist or Engineer

A project of the National Science Foundation, this site puts you in touch with real scientists and engineers who can lend their wealth of experience to your questions about the world.

http://www.nsf.gov/od/lpa/nstw/quests/start.htm

Blue Skies

Check out this special software through the Weather Underground. Called Blue Skies, it allows you to view and manipulate interactive weather maps.

http://groundhog.sprl.umich.edu

The Body Home Page

A site with information and resources for AIDS patients and their families and friends.

http://www.thebody.com

Children's Care Hospital & School

Many children attend school at the hospital if they are there for a long time. Visit this site to learn more about the challenges these kids face.

http://www.cchs.org/kids.html

Convomania

Convomania provides an "OK" place to not be "OK." When you are hurt or sick, this is the place to come for friends and fun.

http://www.mania.apple.com

Dan's Wild Wild Weather Page

Dan Satterfield is the weather guy for WHNT-TV, Channel 19, in Huntsville, Alabama. He brings together great information about all kinds of weather patterns and events.

http://www.whnt19.com/kidwx/index.html

Deaf CyberKids

This is a place to share ideas and feelings about being deaf. This site includes information for subscribing to a DEAFKIDS listserv.

http://dww.deafworldweb.org/kids

Food and Drug Administration

This site is for information about medicines and food quality.

http://www.fda.gov

Food and Drug Administration's Teen Scene

Get information about a variety of health issues that affect teens, particularly drug-related health problems.

http://www.fda.gov/opacom/7teens.html

Family Village

Look here for a large collection of disability-related resources.

http://familyvillage.wisc.edu

Healthfinder

This site can connect you to great resources and information.

http://www.healthfinder.gov

How You Can Help

Want to volunteer your time and energy to helping kids with diseases and disabilities? Use this list of charities to find the group you would most like to work with and then link to that group's own Web site.

http://www.educational.net/charity.htm

Institute of Global Environment and Society Weather Page

Here you can get maps, forecasts, data (updated every hour), and three-day predictions.

http://grads.iges.org/pix/wxmaps.html

Intellicast

If you want to know about weather events, this is the place to go.

http://www.intellicast.com

Kids Did This!

The Franklin Institute Science Museum maintains this collection of links to projects in all kinds of subject areas done by kids and teens. Find ideas for school projects of your own or just see what other people are doing.

http://sln.fi.edu/tfi/hotlists/kids.html

Kids' Home at the National Cancer Institute

The place on the Web to connect with kids with all different types of cancer.

http://icic.nci.nig.gov/occdocs/KidsHome.html

Musenet: The Multi-user Science Education Network

This site provides access to a unique educational experience on the Internet.

http://www.musenet.org

NASA Spacelink

This Web site will give you a glimpse of what is happening inside the space program.

http://spacelink.msfc.nasa.gov

NASA's K-12 Weather Page

Learn more about the weather from the folks who see it all from high above the Earth.

http://www.athena.ivv.nasa.gov/curric/weather/index.html

NASA's Ocean Color Seen from Space

This is NASA's collection of informative satellite photos and other images that illustrate how dynamic and full of life the ocean is, giving you lots of clues to how weather behaves as it crosses the water.

http://www.athena.ivv.nasa.gov/curric/oceans/ocolor/index.html

National Climatic Data Center

This Telnet site contains up-to-the-minute information on hurricanes.

```
telnet://hurricane.ncdc.noaa.gov
```

National Science Foundation's Geoscience Data Server

This Web site has information on all things terrestrial—from seismic (earthquake) data to tides to weather.

```
http://atm.geo.nsf.gov
```

University of California's Museum of Paleontology

This site has the collection from the museum including a great collection of dinosaurs.

```
http://ucmp.berkeley.edu
```

USA Today Weather

Everything you need to know about today's weather can be found here for the United States. You can also send a specific question to the weather editor of the paper and Web site.

```
http://usatoday.com/weather/wfront.htm
```

The Weather Channel Online

The Weather Channel Online gives you local forecasts and other data on cities around the world.

```
http://www.weather.com
```

Weather Underground

Here you can find lots of weather-related information and activities aimed at a K-12 audience.

`http://groundhog.sprl.umich.edu`

World Wide Web Tide Predictor

This online tide calculator is a terrific resource for studying and predicting how the ocean's tides will affect coastal cities all over the world.

`http://tbone.biol.sc.edu/tide/sitesel.html`

Search Tools

AltaVista

If you want to access the most comprehensive index on the Web, check this site out. However, you may get more than you want and it takes a long time to sift through the many sites it will list for you.

`http://www.altavista.digital.com`

Excite

This search tool allows you to do keyword searches as well as follow category or subject links. It also lets you customize your own page of information!

`http://www.excite.com`

HotBot

This search engine speeds through a large and comprehensive data-base of Web sites. Try it and see what you get!

```
http://www.hotbot.com
```

Infoseek

This is a quality search tool that provides a good set of subjects by which to search. It also has fantastic street maps and city guides.

```
http://www.infoseek.com
```

Lycos

In addition to giving you plenty of sites from which to choose, it also has identified the top 5 percent Web sites to help you find places that are well-organized and full of great information.

```
http://www.lycos.com
```

Magellan

When you ask Magellan to find sites for you, it does so and provides you with a great description of what you'll find if you go there.

```
http://www.magellan.com
```

Too Cool for Grownups

Among other things, this site has an overview of all the search engines and what each one can do for you to imporve your Web surfing.

```
http://www.tcfg.com/racers.html
```

WebCrawler

WebCrawler started as a student project and is now managed by American Online. It has a top 100 sites list and is pretty easy to use.

```
http://www.webcrawler.com
```

Yahoo!

This search engine is really an index of sites that are organized around categories. Great place to start a search.

```
http://www.yahoo.com
```

Yahooligans!

This is the side of Yahoo! that applies to kids. Organized the same way but with links to sites that kids find fun, entertaining and informative.

```
http://www.yahooligans.com
```

Sports and Hobbies

Acme Pets Page

For lovers of all kinds of pets.

```
http://www.acmepet.com/index.html
```

The Birder Home Page

Birds, those singing dinosaurs of the air, make for fascinating study. If you're an expert or a beginner, you'll enjoy this page.

```
http://www.birder.com
```

Cool Kids with Clubs

Want to swing a club like Tiger Woods? Contact Steve Jubb: golf pro expert.

```
http://www.pga.com/2
```

Fat Cat Café

Talk to other kids about your hobby. Make trades, learn new tricks, meet new friends.

```
http://www.fatcatcafe.com/kid/hobby
```

The Iditarod Dog Sled Race

Check out this amazing dog sled race across the Alaskan Arctic.

```
http://www.iditarod.org
```

The Internet Base Camp

Tie in and check out this site, which is packed with information and has links to other resources.

```
http://www.concentric.net/~Foxsfca
```

Juggling Information Service

Even jugglers have a site; this one will tell you more then you ever wanted to know about juggling.

```
http://www.juggling.org
```

National Basketball Championships

Check out the action in the NBA during the championships and throughout the season.

http://www.nba.com

Wimbledon Tennis Championships

Here you can learn more about the world's most prestigious tennis tournament.

http://www.wimbledon.org

Women's National Basketball Championships

Here you can learn more about the women's basketball league and championships.

http://www.wnba.com

Yahooligans! Hobbies Index

Yahooligans!, an index of Internet resources for kids, has compiled a list of good sites devoted to hobbies.

http://www.yahooligans.com/Sports_and_Recreation/Hobbies

Appendix B

Glossary of Terms

In this glossary, terms in bold are included in the glossary as well.

Symbols

$0.02

Appended to the end of a Usenet **post** or e-mail message, this means "my two cents."

:-)

The characters for the basic smiley symbol; this is often used to mean "just kidding," "don't flame me," or "I'm being sarcastic," but it can also mean "I'm happy." See also **smileys**.

]

This garbage symbol may appear on your screen, or in text-transferred files, from time to time. It's an uninterpreted Escape character. Ignore it.

a cappella

This is music in which the only instruments used are voices.

acceptable use

Internet service providers require that all users agree to some guidelines of the proper use of Internet and Usenet resources. Acceptable use guidelines vary from provider to provider.

account

A form of access to a computer or **network** for a specific **user name** and password, usually with a home directory, an e-mail inbox, and a set of access privileges.

address

1. The name of a computer (also called a **host** or **site** on the **Internet**, in the form `host.subdomain.domain`. 2. An **e-mail** address in the form `username@host.subdomain.domain`. 3. A **Web** address (**URL**) in the form `http://host.subdomain.domain/optionalpath/optional-filename.html`.

address book

In some **e-mail** programs, a list of abbreviations for e-mail addresses.

alias

An abbreviation for an **e-mail address**, sometimes called a nickname.

altitude

The vertical distance of a city from sea level.

application

A computer program (or piece of software) that isn't a shell, environment, or operating system. Examples include Web browsers, word processing programs, and spreadsheet programs.

article

A posting to a **Usenet** group.

ASCII

American Standard Code for Information Interchange; ASCII is a standard character set that's been adopted by most computer systems around the world.

ASCII file

A file containing only plain text. ASCII files are easier and quicker to transfer.

asynchronous

Not happening at the same time. E-mail is an asynchronous form of communication.

attachment

Any data file, in any form, that your e-mail program will send along with your e-mail message.

back

In a Web browser this is a shortcut button, for retracing your steps to the previous page or link.

baud

Usually confused with bps (bits per second), baud is technically the number of times per second that your **modem** changes the signal it sends through the phone lines.

Bcc line

The portion of an e-mail message header where you list the recipients who will be sent blind copies of an e-mail. This means that the primary (and Cc:) recipients will not see the names of people receiving blind copies.

binary transfer

A file transfer in which every bit of the file is copied (as opposed to a text transfer, in which the text is transferred to whatever format the receiving machine prefers).

BinHex

A form of file compression native to the Macintosh computer.

bookmark

In a Web browser, a record of a destination that allows you to immediately get back there at any time. (Also called Favorites or Favorite Places in some browsers, and Items on a Hotlist in others.)

bounce

When e-mail fails to reach its destination and returns to you, it is said to have bounced.

bps

Acronymn for "bits per second"; a measurement of modem speed.

brain teaser

A thinking game that is a puzzle.

browse

To skim an information resource on the Net, such as **Gopher** or the **Web**.

browser

The program you use to explore the **Web**.

BTW

Acronymn for "by the way," a phrase used often in **e-mail**.

bulletin board

1. What some online services call their discussion groups. 2. A **bulletin board system**.

bulletin board system (or BBS)

A set of computers and modems running bulletin board software that allow users to dial in, send mail, participate in forums, and (sometimes) access the Internet.

bureaus

Remote offices; usually used to describe news offices around the world.

chat

Synchronous, line-by-line communication over a network. A means to communicate with others through the Internet, just as you would talk to someone on the telephone except you are each typing what you want to say.

client

An application that communicates with a server to get you information.

client-server application

An application whose process is distributed between a central server and any number of autonomous clients.

.com

An Internet **domain** that stands for "commercial."

COM port

A communication port in your computer. Your modem plugs into one.

commands

Common sayings that are typed into a computer program or game to execute an action.

commercial online service

A private, proprietary network offering its own content and access to other network members, such as CompuServe, America Online, and the Microsoft Network.

comp.

A **Usenet** hierarchy devoted to computers.

compress

To squish, or reduce the size of, a file so that it can be sent easier and faster over the Internet.

compression

The method of reducing the size of a file or the amount of squishing.

copyright

A legal right that restricts other people's usage of a person's original material without the author's permission. People debate how standing copyright law applies texts in general made available on the Internet. Some people attach copyright notices to their posts. See also **fair use**.

correspondent

A person who you communicate with.

CU-SeeMe

A protocol that enables anyone with a video camera and enough memory to play video images in their computer to see other people on the Internet and other people see them at the same time.

data bits

One of the things you have to set to use your modem. Usually set to 7 or 8, it depends on the modem you're calling.

database

A large collection of information that is searchable.

decoding

Retranslating a file from some encoded format to its original format.

decrypt

To remove the encryption from a file or e-mail message and make it readable.

dial-up account

An Internet account on a **host** machine that you must dial up with your modem to use.

Direct-Access ISP

An **Internet service provider** (usually called an ISP) that offers direct Internet access, as opposed to a commercial online service.

directory

A Web site where links to other Web sites are organized by topic and subtopic, something like a Yellow Pages phone book.

discussion groups

Any "place" on the Net where discussions are held, including mailing lists and Usenet newsgroups.

domain

The three-letter code indicating whether the address is a business (.com), a non-profit (.org), a university (.edu), a branch of the government (.gov), a part of the military (.mil), and so on.

download

To transfer a file over a modem from a remote computer to your desktop computer.

.edu

An Internet domain that stands for "educational."

e-mail

Electronic mail, but you knew that already, didn't you?

e-mail address

An Internet address that consists of a **user name** (also called a login, a log-on name, a userID, an account name, and so on), followed by an "at" sign (@) and then an address of the form host@subdomain.domain.

encoding

Any method of converting a file into a format for attaching to e-mail messages.

encrypt

To scramble the contents of a file or e-mail message so that only those with the key can unscramble and read them.

encryption

A process of rendering a file or e-mail message unreadable to anyone lacking the right encryption key.

Eudora

An **e-mail** program.

fair use

The legal doctrine that allows limited quotation of other people's work if the use of their work does not undercut its market value.

FAQ

1. Acronymn for "frequently asked questions." 2. A file containing frequently asked questions and their answers, also sometimes called a FAQL (Frequently Asked Question List).

field research

Going out into the wilderness and observing the behavior of the object of your study.

file transfer

To copy a file from one computer to another.

flame

An ill-considered, insulting e-mail or Usenet retort.

flame war

Prompted by one **flame** message, other participants on a listserv or Usenet group submit flame messages back to the flame's original author.

FOAF

Acronymn for "friend of a friend."

follow a link

In graphical browsers, following a **link** entails positioning the mouse pointer over the link (the pointer will change to show you that you're over an active link) and then clicking once.

forms

Forms allow you to type information right on your browser screen as you're looking at the Web, just as you would on a paper form. The information you put into the form, which looks like a series of boxes on the page, is then sent through the Internet like e-mail to the host of the Web site.

frames

Frames divide your browser screen into sections, each with its own HTML source and scroll tabs. Often you'll see frames used for navigation, so that you can click on a link in one frame and see the information you wanted in the other frame.

freeware

Free software available for downloading on the Net.

FTP

Acronymn for "File Transfer Protocol," the standard Internet way to transfer files from one computer to another.

FTP site

A computer on the Net containing archives and set up for **FTP.**

FTPmail

A way to use FTP by e-mail if you don't have an **FTP** application.

FWIW

Acronymn meaning "for what it's worth."

`<g>`

Indicates the author is grinning, similar to :-). See **smileys**.

garbage characters

Nonsense characters that modems sometimes spit out.

GIF

1. A compressed graphics (image) file format (GIF stands for graphics interchange format) invented by CompuServe. 2. A file in the .gif format.

Gopher

A client-server application that performs **FTP** transfers, remote logins, archie searches, and so on, presenting everything to you in the form of menus. This saves you from having to know (or type in) the addresses of the Internet resources being tapped. You run a Gopher client program to get information from a Gopher server running at a Gopher site.

Gopherspace

A collective name for all the **Gopher** servers on the Net, so called because all the servers can connect to each other, creating a unified "space" of Gopher menus.

.gov

An Internet domain that stands for "government."

graphical user interface (GUI)

A GUI uses pictures and icons, rather than just words, to display Web sites.

<grin>

Equivalent to the :-) smiley.

group

A newsgroup.

home page

1. The page you begin with when you start your Web browser. 2. The main page of a Web site. 3. A personal Web page.

host

A computer on the Internet.

HotJava

A Web browser made by Sun Microsystems.

hotlist

A **bookmark** list of favorite Web sites.

HTML

Acronymn for "Hypertext Markup Language"; the hypertext language used to create Web pages. It consists of regular text and tags that tell the browser application what to do when a link is activated.

HTML source

The underlying source file that makes a Web document look the way it does in a Web browser.

HTTP

Acronymn for "Hypertext Transfer Protocol"; the Web protocol for linking one Web page with another.

hypermedia

Linked documents that consist of other media in addition to plain text, such as pictures, sounds, movies, and so on.

hypertext

Text that contains links to other text documents.

hypertext link

A link from one text document to another.

image file

A binary file. A format for a file containing pictures, photos, or graphics.

IMHO

Acronym for "in my humble opinion."

IMNSHO

Acronym for "in my not-so-humble opinion."

IMO

Acronym for "in my opinion."

inbox

A file containing your incoming e-mail.

info

Many Internet providers have an info address (`info@host.subdomain`
`.domain`).

Internet

The worldwide network of networks. The Internet is a way for computers to communicate with each other.

Internet address

See **address**.

Internet Explorer

Microsoft's Web browser application.

Internet Phone

A protocol that enables anyone with a microphone, speaker, and sound card in their computer to talk to other people on the Internet.

Internet service provider (ISP)

A company that offers just access to the Internet and no local content (or only very limited local information and discussion groups).

IP

Acronymn for "Internet Protocol"; the protocol that allows computers and networks on the Internet to communicate with each other.

IRC

Acronymn for "Internet Relay Chat"; a protocol and a client-server program that allows you to chat with people all over the Internet, in channels devoted to different topics.

Ircle

A Macintosh IRC program.

Java

A programming language from Sun Microsystems that's a variant of the C++ programming language. With Java-savvy browsers, users can interact with fully operational programs inside of the browser window.

JPEG

A compressed file format for images with the extension .jpg. JPEG stands for Joint Photographic Experts Group, who invented the format.

k12.

A Usenet hierarchy devoted to kindergarten through 12th grade education.

keyword

A word used to search for a file, document, or Web page.

kps

Kilobits (or a thousand bits) per second, a measurement of **modem** speed.

LAN

Acronymn for a "local-area network." A computer network usually confined to a single office or building.

latitude

A city's distance, measured in degrees, from the equator, the line which separates the Northern and Southern Hemispheres. See also **longitude**.

library catalogs

Many university and public library catalogs are available via the Web.

link

On Web pages, a button or highlighted bit of text that, when selected, jumps the reader to another page or Web site.

list

Usually refers to a mailing list.

listserv

A type of mailing list that operates through e-mail.

local-area network

A small, local network, such as in an office (LAN).

log in

To start a session on your Internet account.

login

A user name, the name you log in with.

log out

To end a session on your Internet account.

LOL

Acronymn for "laughing out loud."

longitude

A city's distance, measured in degrees, from the prime meridian, an imaginary vertical line that runs through Greenwich, England. See also **latitude**.

lurk

To read a mailing list or newsgroup without posting to it. You should lurk for a while before posting.

lurker

One who **lurk**s.

mail

On the Internet, synonymous with e-mail.

mail box

A folder or area in a mail program where messages are stored.

mailing list

A list of people with a common interest, all of whom receive all the mail sent, or posted, to the list.

mail reader

A program that allows you to read and reply to e-mail, and to send out new mail of your own.

message

1. An e-mail letter. 2. A comment sent to a specific person on **IRC** (Internet Relay Chat) and not to the entire channel.

meteorology

The study of weather.

MIDI

Acronymn for "Musical Instrument Digital Interface." This device allows you to compose music digitally and store and edit it inside the computer.

MIME

Acronymn for "Multipurpose Internet Mail Extensions," a protocol that allows e-mail to contain more than simple text. Used to send other kinds of data, including color pictures, sound files, and video clips.

.mil

An Internet domain that stands for "military."

mIRC

A Windows IRC program.

mirror site

Another FTP site that maintains the exact same files (updated regularly), in order to reduce the load on the primary site.

misc.

A Usenet hierarchy devoted to whatever doesn't fit in the other hierarchies.

modem

A device that connects your computer to a phone jack and, through the phone lines, to another modem and computer. (It stands for modulator/ demodulator.)

moderated

Lists and newsgroups whose posts, or posted messages, must pass muster with a moderator before being sent to the subscribers.

moderator

The volunteer who decides which submissions to a moderated list or newsgroup will be posted.

Mosaic

A Web browser, developed by NCSA, for graphical user interfaces.

MPEG

A compressed file format for movies with the extension .mpg.

MUD

Acronym for a "multiuser domain/dimension/dungeon." A role-playing game environment that allows people all over the Net to play together in something like interactive text adventures.

MUSE

Acronymn for a "multiuser simulation environment" (for role-playing games).

Net, the

Often used as an abbreviation for the **Internet**, the Net is really a more general term for the lump sum of interconnected computers on the planet.

.net

An Internet domain that stands for network.

netiquette

The traditional rules of civilized behavior online.

Netscape Navigator

A popular World Wide Web browser program.

network

A linked-together set of computers and computer equipment. The Internet is a worldwide network.

newbie

A beginner on the Net.

newsfeed

The packet of news articles passed along from one computer to the next on Usenet.

newsgroup

A Usenet discussion group.

.newsrc

The list of subscribed and unsubscribed newsgroups for a Unix newsreader.

newsreader

A program used to read Usenet articles.

NIC

Acronymn for a "network information center."

node

Any computer on the Internet, a host.

noise

Useless or unwanted information (as in signal-to-noise ratio).

offline

Not currently connected to the Net.

offline mail reader

A mail program that connects to the Net, downloads your e-mail, and then disconnects, allowing you to read, reply to, and send mail without being charged for very much connect time (except for the time spent downloading the e-mail messages).

offline news reader

A newsreader that connects to the Net, downloads all unread articles in all subscribed newsgroups, and then disconnects, allowing you to read, reply to, and post articles without being charged for connect time.

online

Currently connected to the Net.

.org

An Internet domain that stands for non-profit "organization."

page

A hypertext document available on the World Wide Web.

parent directory

The parent for which the current **directory** is a subdirectory.

parity

One of the things you have to set to use your **modem**. It's usually set to None or Even, but it depends on the modem you're calling.

phenomena

Events that happen.

platform

A type of computer or system.

players

Programs, also called viewers, used to display multimedia file formats.

plug-ins

Programs that can be plugged into, or added to, a Web browser to add multimedia capabilities to it.

point at

To start a client program; such as a Web **browser**, by supplying it with an address, as in "Point your Web browser at `http://www.exploratorium.edu` to see the latest exhibit in the Exploratorium."

POP

1. Acronym for "Point of Presence"; a local access number for a service provider; 2. Post-Office Protocol, a standard way to download and upload **e-mail**.

POP server

A type of mail server that "speaks" the Post-Office Protocol.

post

To send a message to a mailing list or an article to a newsgroup. The word "post" comes from the bulletin-board metaphor, in which scraps of paper are posted to the board, to be read by anyone.

Postmaster

The person responsible for information requests for a mail server (postmaster@address).

PPP

An acronym for "Point-to-Point Protocol"; a protocol for an Internet connection over a **modem**.

precipitation

Rain or moisture.

query

A search request submitted to a **database**.

queue

A list of messages waiting to be sent.

QuickTime

A movie format originally on Macintoshes.

Real Audio

Progressive Networks' streaming audio format. Allows Web browsers to play audio without downloading files.

real name

Your full name as it appears on **e-mail** messages and **Usenet** posts.

real time

The time it takes real people to communicate, as on a telephone.

rec.

A Usenet hierarchy devoted to recreation.

remote login

Logging into another computer over a **network**. See also **Telnet**.

reply

An e-mail message or Usenet post responding to, and possibly quoting, the original.

repost

To post again. A subsequent post of the same information.

ROTFL

Acronymn for "rolling on the floor laughing."

scatting

A musical technique of using nonsensical words and phrases in an effort to create the illusion of many instruments.

sci.

A Usenet hierarchy devoted to science.

search engine

A program, usually reachable through a Web page, used to search a Web site, the entire Internet, or some domain in between. Popular search engines include Yahoo!, Excite, Lycos, and others.

server

A network application providing information to client programs that connect to it. They are centralized repositories of information or specialized handlers of certain kinds of traffic.

service provider

A company that provides access to the **Internet**.

shareware

Software that is available for a free trial and must be registered and paid for if you decide to use it.

.sig

A signature file.

signature

A few lines of text, usually including your name, sometimes your postal (snail mail) address, and perhaps your e-mail address. Many people also include quotations, jokes, gags, and so on. Signatures (also called sig blocks, signature files, .signatures, or .sigs) are a little like bumper stickers in this respect. Some e-mail programs do not support signature files.

site

An Internet host that allows some kind of remote access, such as a **Web** site, **Gopher** site, and so on.

smileys

Sideways smiley faces, such as :-), ;^), and = %7o, used to indicate emotions or facial expressions.

SMTP

Simple Mail Transport Protocol; this protocol is what enables Internet e-mail to flow so freely.

snail mail

Internet slang for surface, or normal, mail delivered by the Postal Service.

soc.

A Usenet hierarchy devoted to society.

spam

A term used to describe when someone posts (or roboposts) huge amounts of material to Usenet, or posts one article or message to huge numbers of inappropriate groups.

stanza

A verse in poetry.

stop bits

One of the things you have to set to use your modem. Usually set to 1 or 2, but it depends on the modem you're calling.

storyboard

A sketch of how your Web pages will look and relate to one another in sequence.

streaming

When files are sent a little at a time and start playing almost immediately. Audio files that play immediately without downloading the files use stream-lining technology.

subdirectory

A **directory** that is a subset of another directory.

subdomain

A named portion of an Internet domain, usually a network, university, or company. In the e-mail address, `xian@netcom.com`, netcom is the subdomain.

subscribe

To join a mailing list or start reading a newsgroup.

surf

To **browse**, following tangents or links to other sites on the Web.

synchronous

Happening at the same time. **Chat** is a synchronous form of communication.

sysop

A system operator. Someone who runs or maintains a network.

system administrator

Someone who runs or maintains a network.

system operator

A type of system administrator who runs a BBS.

tablature

Tablature is a system of musical notation used most often for stringed instruments. The lines represent the strings, and the notes or letters on them represent finger placement.

tags

Tags are words and phrases in HTML that tell Web browsers how to display your Web page.

talk

One-to-one synchronous chatting over the Net.

talk.

A **Usenet** hierarchy devoted to discussion, argument, and debate.

TCP

Acronymn for "Transmission Control Protocol"; a protocol that transmits information over the Internet, one small piece at a time.

TCP/IP

The Internet protocol using TCP.

Telnet

A protocol for remote login, and the name of most programs that use that protocol.

text file

A file containing text only.

text transfer

A transfer of straight text over the modem, between the remote computer and your desktop computer.

thread

A series of **post**s and follow-ups in a newsgroup.

threaded newsreader

A **newsreader** that organizes posts according to a **thread** and allows you to read your way up or down a thread.

time out

To fail, as a network process, because the remote server or computer has not responded in time.

TrueSound

Microsoft's own streaming sound format.

TurboGopher

A **Gopher** program for the Mac.

uncompress

To unsquish, or expand, a compressed file to its original form that can be used by an application.

uncompression

The process of unsquishing, or expanding, a file to its original format.

Uniform Resource Locator (URL)

A Web address. It consists of a protocol, a hostname, a port (optional), a directory, and a file name.

Unix

An operating system common to workstations and on which most Internet protocols were developed.

unmoderated

Type of newsgroup or list whose articles are not checked by a moderator.

unsubscribe

To remove yourself from a mailing list or to stop reading a **Usenet** newsgroup.

upload

To transfer a file over a **modem** from your desktop computer to a remote computer.

URL

See **Uniform Resource Locator**.

Usenet

1. The collection of computers and networks that share news articles. Usenet is not the Internet (though they overlap to a great extent); 2. The hierarchy of newsgroups.

user name

Also called a login or userID. The name a user logs in with. Also the first part of your e-mail address (up to the @).

viewers

See **players**.

virus

A program that deliberately does damage to the computer it's on.

.VOC

The audio format for the SoundBlaster sound card.

VRML

Acronymn for "Virtual Reality Modeling Language"; VRML files usually have a .wrl extension.

VT100

A terminal type, originated by DEC, that has become the standard terminal. If you dial up a Unix shell, then your communications program probably emulates a VT100.

WAN

Acronymn for a "wide-area network." A computer **network** spanning a wide geographical area.

.wav

Wave format, from Microsoft; perhaps the most widespread sound format on the Internet.

Web

Short for the **World Wide Web**.

Web address

A **Uniform Resource Locator**.

Web browser

A program, such as Navigator or Internet Explorer, that allows you to view hypertext pages and follow links.

Web page

A hypertext document on the Web.

Web server

A computer that is always turned on and connected to the Internet that stores Web pages and makes them available via **HTTP** (Hypertext Transfer Protocol).

whisper

A private message to someone in an **IRC** session.

WinZip

A compression program for Windows. See also **zip file**.

working directory

The current directory. The directory you're "in" right now.

World Wide Web

A collection of graphical hypertext documents and associated files, linked together, that is part of the Internet (and hence, the globe). Also called the "Web."

Xmodem

A protocol for download and upload file transfers.

zine

Short for an electronic "magazine" on the Net.

zip file

A file that's been compressed to save space or transfer time.

Zmodem

A protocol for download and upload file transfers.

Index

NOTE: Numbers in *italics* indicate a page with a illustration.